COMMERCIAL SPACE

Boutiques

COMMERCIAL SPACE

Boutiques

 arco
editorial

AUTHOR
Francisco Asensio Cerver

EDITOR IN CHIEF
Paco Asensio

PROJECT COORDINATOR
Iván Bercedo (Architect)

TRANSLATION & PROOFREADING
Lawrence Mc Allister

GRAPHIC DESIGN & LAYOUT
Mireia Casanovas Soley

PHOTOGRAPHERS
Paul Warchol (*Jil Sander Paris & Chicago*); Jordi Sarrà (*The End*); Jordi Trallero (*Jean-Pierre Victim's*); Jerry Pair & Associates (*Jerry Pair*); Sigurgeir Sigurjónsson (*Galleri & Eva*); Friedrich Busam & Christoph Kicherer (*One Studio Off*); Francesc Tur (*Dolce & Gabanna (Uomo/ Donna, San Francisco Story*); Dan Forer (*Tempus*); Paul Bielenberg (*Great Hall*); George Cott (*Haggar*); Nacása & Partners Inc. (*Dr. Baeltz*); Joan Mundó (*Josep Font*); Klaus Frahm (*Ocky's*)

Copyright © 1996 Arco Editorial SA
ISBN: 2-88046-282-7

Published and distributed by ROTOVISION SA
Sheridan House
112-116A Western Road
Hove, East Sussex BN3 1DD
England
Tel. 1273 72 72 68
Fax 1273 72 72 69

Production and color separation in Singapore by
ProVision Pte. Ltd.
Tel: (065) 334-7720
Fax: (065) 334-7721

Foodstuffs, cleaning products, household appliances, household items, tools, there exists a progressive tendency to concentrate the sale of a wide range of products at hypermarkets and department stores. The criteria for doing this are mainly economic; uniting a wide range of products reduces costs for the seller and saves time for the shopper. However, the world of fashion or perfume seems to come up against continual obstacles when the same type of approach is tried in this area. On the other hand, in a lot of fashion shops a direct relation between the client and the product is not facilitated. The client should fit in to the scene that the designer or the architect has created for the boutique and participate in a certain atmosphere created with images before trying on the displayed items for sale. In a lot of cases he or she will be accompanied by an assistant who will give advice and explain the characteristics of the clothes. Well-known firms and famous brands have gradually replaced the dressmaker or tailor, but continue to need to feel part of a singular, different and recognisable aesthetics. Even the clothes departments of department stores are usually sub-divided into different sections. Homogeneity dilutes all that we feel that a jacket, dress or shirt should concord with our personality. The case of perfume is clear. Although the perfume does not have a physical image, often more an image rather than a fragrance is sold. A scene is created from the scent associated with a world of references and associations in which the would-be buyer is invited to participate. The design of the scenery is thus of primary importance. The aesthetics of a firm is not only limited to the design of clothes or a scent bottle, but also involves the architecture of the shops as well as marketing. It is a question of what is called brand image. Along these lines, if the buyer wants to buy a garment that is suited to his or her personal taste, he or she also wishes to purchase something that denotes the company behind the product. It is basically the same as the work done by a famous painter. Although each painting can be understood as an independent piece, in many cases what gives a special value to a painting is its capacity to show essential themes in the career of the artist. In this volume, we have wished to compile examples from highly different places; from Japan to Italy or from The United States to Iceland. Our aim is to offer the reader a panorama of different examples. Along these lines, we may state that the problems that the designers faced and the answers they came up with are very different in each one of the cases. The reduced dimensions of the Dr Baeltz or Dolce & Gabbana shops contrast with the size of Jill Sanders' boutique in Paris, The End in Ibiza or the Great Mall in California. The young, sporty look of the clothes that are sold in Tempus or Haggar is completely different to the minimalist style and content of Josep Font. This diversity of

situations turns into a variety of solutions that enrich the book. For the same reason, we have also wanted to include boutiques specialised in other types of products; perfumes in the case of Dr. Baeltz, shoes in Eva Company or furniture in One Studio Off or Atlanta Decorative Arts Center. More than the ingenious solutions in construction or the choice of materials and finishes, we show that each project entails a compromise of the architect with a certain philosophy that the firm tries to express. The first decision of the project and the most important is to know how to translate this spirit into architectural terms. The most difficult, but also the most attractive.

Boutiques

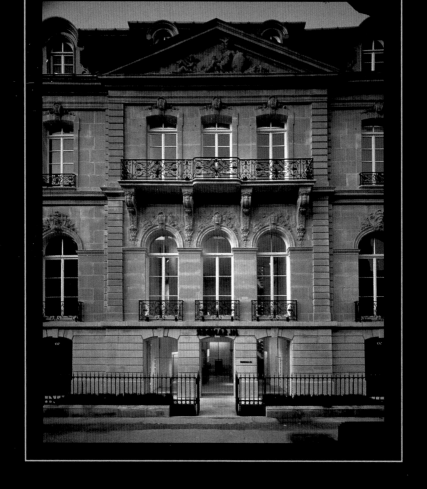

▲ The nineteenth-century limesone façade has been retored as the shop front for a boutique. Sound-proofed glass windows let in natural light from the north. Interior lighting of the double space shows off the façade.

► The furniture and mannequins are like small cubic objects and set off the vast space where the old exists with

The location chosen by the firm of the German designer Jil Sander for its debut in Paris is an old palace situated at number 52 of the distinguished Avenue Montaigne.

Built in 1890, it was a private home that exemplified the Beaux-Arts tradition of French architecture and in 1923 it became the fashion centre for Madeleine Vionnet.

During the seventies, the building was acquired by Phillips Electronics to hold its headquarters in France. The most recent owners (ARC Union) purchased the house in 1990 and planned to pull it down. It was at this point that the façade became listed as a monument of interest for the city of Paris.

Gabellini introduces a new order that establishes a new dialogue between the architectural heritage of the construction and its recent changes (a modern, anonymous structure of four floors, one of which is a

▲ *On the second floor, the lighting in the ceiling and a black granite bench run parallel to the façade. (C1)*

▶ *Above the granite bench, next to the façade, black ebony shelves are laid out. (C2)*

▶ *View of the interior through one of the openings in the façade. The separation between the side wall and the stairs means that part of the latter can be seen.*

▲ ▶ *Views from the back part of the first floor towards the façade.(B3)*

▲ *On the first floor the contrast between the well-lit white space and the black ebony from Macasar is seen.(B1)*

▶ *On the following page, an axonometric projection. On the ground floor the three vertical columns that delimit the space stand out.*

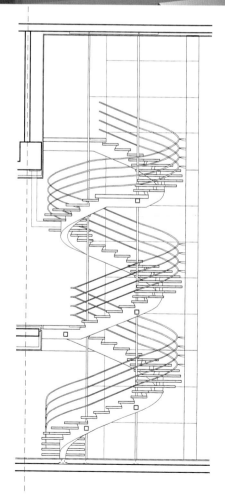

▶ *Section of the stairs.*

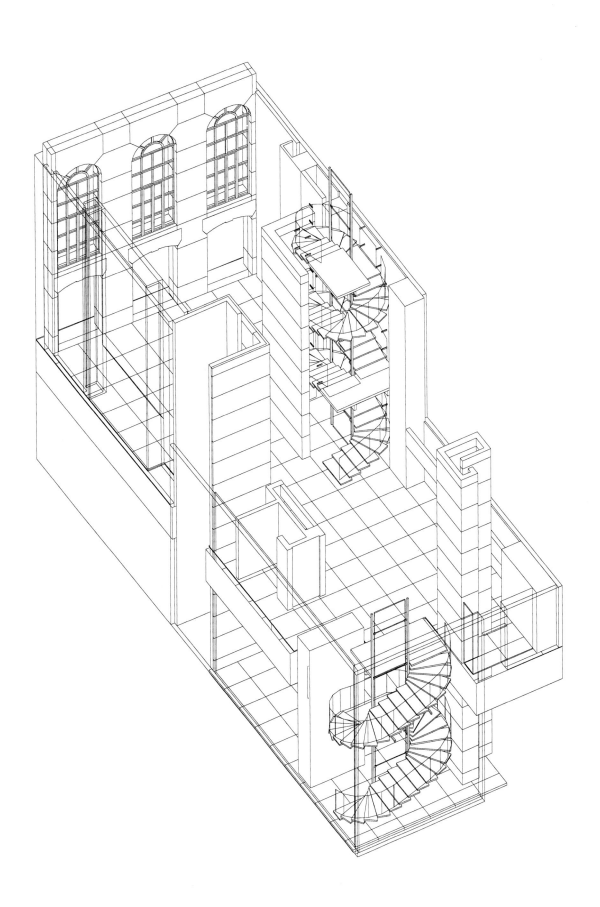

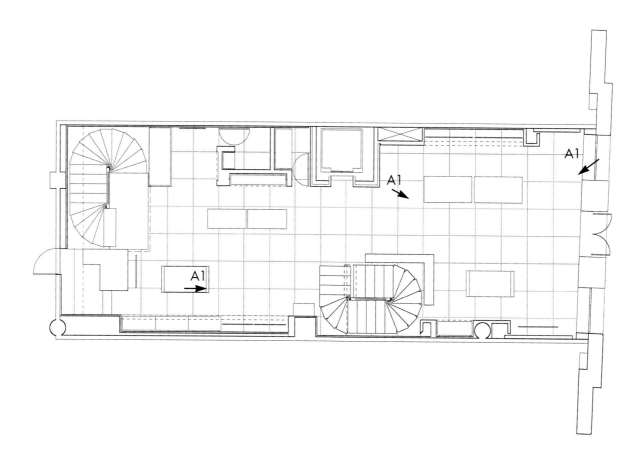

▲ Ground floor.

▼ First floor. The stairs protrude out into the space
next to the entrance.

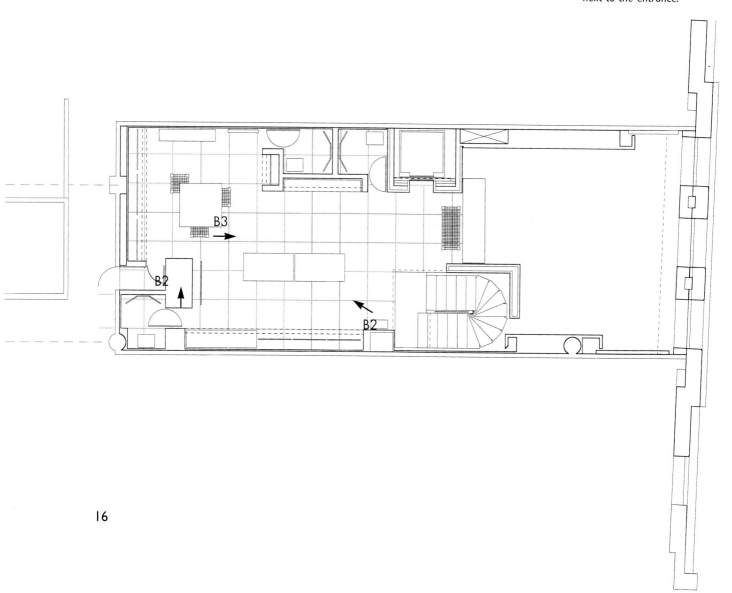

delimiting the ample space of the entrance. These towers contain the stairs and the lift and, while they are joined by a balcony, one is slightly further forward than the other.

Gabellini and his consultant, Johnson Schwinghammer, came up with a theatrical lighting system for the project. A system of sensors set up on the façade monitors daylight and adjusts the interior lighting on the different floors.

The lower part of the side walls have recesses in which shelves and hangers are fitted. The recesses form a mysterious background of light for display of the products.

At the end of the ground floor, a third

▼ *The limestone steps of the stairs seem to float and are fixed by a spiral of wrought iron. The lacquer on the ironwork has been especially designed by Gabellini.*

▲ *Opposite the entrance two white marble monolithic "columns" rise up. A balcony spans the space between them. Behind, the light of new spaces. (A3)*

basement). The most important decision was to get rid of 40% of the fittings of the ground floor to create a double entrance space open to the street with the air of a court. The historical façade is thus revealed as well as its interior with its limestone finish.

Jil Sanders describes her clothes, perfumes and accessories as being elegant, classic, subtle and forceful. Qualities which could also define the impression one receives on entering the shop. Two columns, finished in the same white marble as the floor, rise up next to the side walls

◄ View of the basement.

▼ The second floor reaches the façade and extends towards the east. The stairs and the lift provide an intersection between the three levels.

▼ The space is filled with light. The lighting softens the space converting it into a whitish mist.

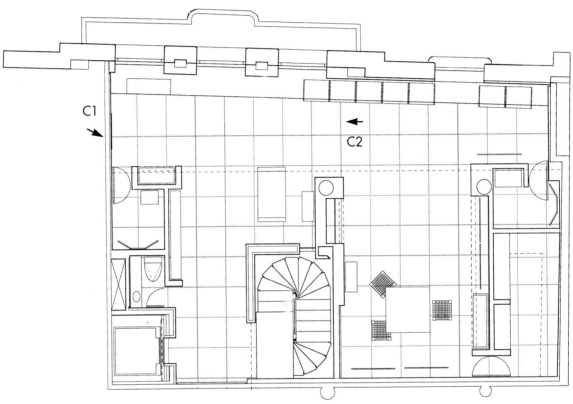

C1

C2

marble element is seen that shields the rear entrance and delimits the fitting rooms of the upper floor and a sales till on the lower floor.

The finish of the façade, the delimiting of the space through marble columns next to the walls, the lighting and the choice of materials and furniture defines an elegant space that recalls the words that Jil Sander describes her work with "... when it is worn, it hangs like an angel around the body". ■

▲ The spiral of the stairs provides a dynamic link between the three floors. In the background, on the other side of the balcony, the façade with its characteristic openings and its ochre limestone tone. (B3)

The seating area of the first floor. The table is black granite and the chairs are natural Nogal wood from Greece with intertwined leather straps. (B2)

JIL SANDER (Chicago)

Michael Gabellini

▲ *View of the entrance façade; a simple opening with the entrance towards the corner, together with the name of the firm on the marble.*

► *The mannequins, always on a white background, interplay with the planes which lay out the shop. To the left, one of the translucent doors of the fitting rooms.*

Michael Gabellini worked as an architect for six years for the New York firm Kohn Pedersen Fox Associates (KPF). He collaborated in the design and construction of different high-rise buildings in America and Europe and in 1987 he set up his own company. The designs of Gabellini Associates, especially aimed at the boutiques, exhibition rooms, residential projects and furniture are denoted by their simplicity and select use of materials. His work has received numerous prizes and recognition, among which stand out the American Institute of Architect's Medallion Award for his boutique-exhibition hall in Paris for the firm Jil Sander.

A year after opening her first shop ouside Germany, Jil Sander opened a new establishment. It often happens that prestigious firms in the world of fashion try to find the same image for all of their shops, the design of which is trusted to an architect. Michael Gabellini again designs a Sander boutique, this time on the ground floor of a building in the city of Chicago.

The difference between the two shops is fundamentally due to their previous existence. Differences in the proportion of the floor and the treatment of the façade. The façade becomes a plain marble frame and its opening, completely glazed, becomes a shop window for the interior space. The same pieces of furniture are repeated, the same materials, the same illuminated recesses on the white walls which display the same clothes. But the space

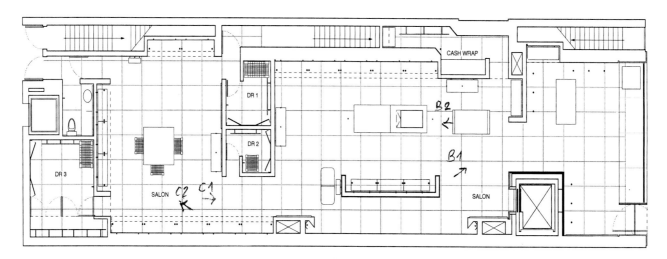

◄ A sequence of illuminated planes and different dark objects attracts with force and simplicity. (C2)

◄ The street from within the abstract interior world of the shop becomes a stage of daily life. The mysterious lighting creates almost magical spaces in which walls and furniture are united. (B1)

◄ The ground floor. A rectangular space with a longitudinal character. The use of the walls is fundamental. The lay-out of the lift, the fitting rooms and the partitions and furniture creates an interesting diversity of areas.

▲ The clothes stand out on the purity of the illuminated white walls and contrast with black ebony. In the background, a new space is hinted at. (B2)

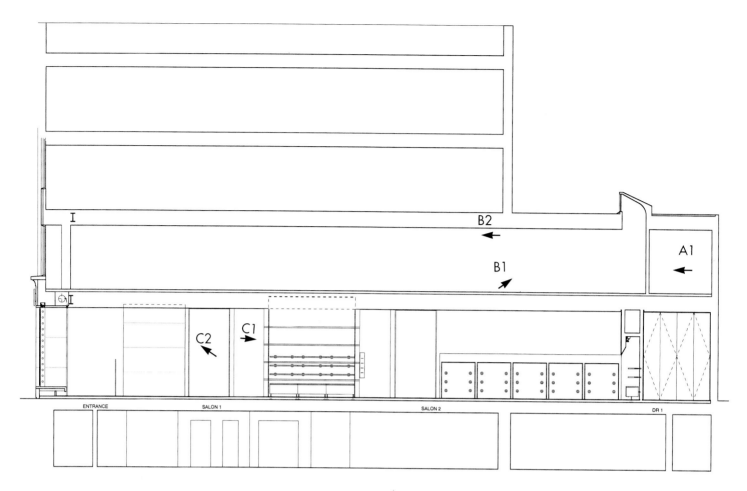

▲ *Longitudinal section.*

is always different. The greater floor surface and its more elongated shape made Gabellini think deeply. The same resources are repeated, but other resources appear.

The depth of the marble frame leads through to the entrance and delimits what seems to be an empty shop window; a dark granite step next to the pavement. Through the glass, one's look spreads out over the space filled with light, looking for the end of the homogenous space with recesses and cavities that is flecked by black objects.

Appendices surge out from the side walls, such as the lift, or the fitting rooms that allow one to differentiate the areas of the shop; in the central area a partition in the shape of a "C" creates new alternatives and the white walls provide illuminated recesses to hold the clothes.

Michael Gabellini describes Jil Sanders' clothes as "clean elegance". The white interiors that he has created for her shops could be defined as the architectural expression of the same idea. What also should be added, perhaps, is the magic that results when light turns out to be a synonym for space. ■

▼ *In the interior, the white of the plaster predominates over the marble of the floor, dotted by metallic details such as the hangers or the door of the lift and the natural or black wood of the furniture.*

THE END

Eduard Samsó

▲ *Details of the claret velvet fitting rooms.
They appear as curtains which magicians use
to make people disappear.*

▶ *A monochromatic interior, both
warm and soft, in which various materials
define limits. The dark colours used for some
items stand out on to which bars, lights and
objects are fitted. (A1)*

Number 26 of "La Calle de la Cruz" was a typical fisherman's house hidden in the old quarter of Ibiza next to the port. This terraced house is quite long with two entrances at each of its ends.

Eduard Samso was commisioned to turn the premises into a suitable place to sell clothes. The fashion shop, The End, required a completely different layout to that existing which entailed the complete removal of all of the inside of the house. At the same time the stone arches on the ground floor, the Mares stone of the supporting walls and the wooden structure of the roof were considered to be appropriate for the new function of the house. The external appearance and the character of the façade were also kept in an effort to maintain the house in line with the character of the old quarter of Ibiza. The removal of the interior should then be considered as refurbishing the house for its new purpose.

The house is located perpendicularly to the port. The two façades have balconies on the upper floor with small windows. The entrance from the street is outlined by a golden frame in which the logo of the shop is seen. Openings in the façade show off its thickness and sturdiness. The shop functions as a longitudinal space between the street and the seafront with a door at each end. On entering, through either door, all of the ground floor is seen divided up into five galleries by the arches. The use of grained marble defines both entrances. It reaches halfway up the wall in the interior of the façades and continues as flooring to create the steps, three from the seafront and one from the street, which go down to the parquet of the three central galleries.

The wooden flooring has the same warm clear tone as that of the walls and arches. Some of the furniture also adds to the

The hangers and bars are like gateways of pillars and girders which subtly offer the merchandise that hangs from them" (Eduard Samsó).

Metallic bars hang from the ceiling tracing zig-zags on which the oval rings of the fitting rooms are suspended. Other straight bars at different angles support spotlights. (B1)

monochromatic atmosphere in which the fitting rooms and the stairs stand out.

The fitting rooms are three curtains which hang from oval rings which in turn hang from a metallic bar in the shape of a zig-zag, which is suspended from the ceiling. The curtains are made in claret velvet and reach the floor.

The stairs are made up of a series of black metallic sections that join and overlap leading the customer to the different levels. The stairs complete with stays and an intermittant handrail is suspended in space rising up to the first floor.

In contrast to the horizontal layout of the ground floor, the stairwell may be defined as a square window which visually and spatially links the three floors of the shop.

Women's wear and the till are located on the ground floor, the middle floor takes in, under a sloping ceiling, men's wear and auxiliary services and lastly on the top floor, consisting of a single gallery, a small office is found.

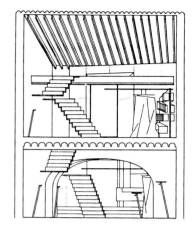

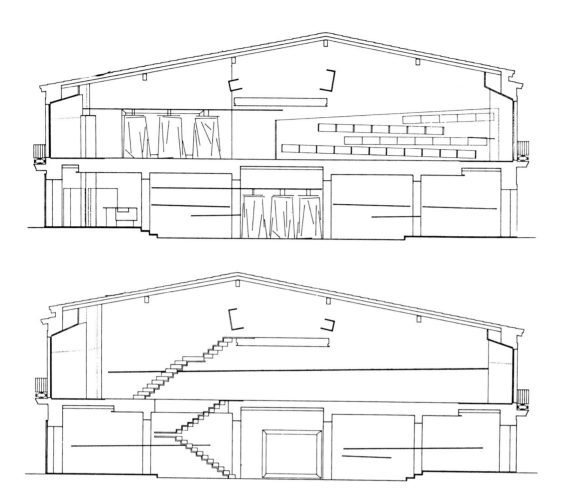

On the middle floor the same decorative materials are used. The use of marble to form a design parallel to the façades and fittings should be pointed out.

The refurbishing of the house creates a space between the ceiling and four walls. The decoration and fittings lets the space escape through the bareness of the walls up to the stairwell to then hide in the façades or in the attic. As if it were a child. ■

▲ *Ground, first and upper floors.*

▲ *The different sections that make up the stairs do not touch. They are like metal tapestries that fold in space. The sections of handrail also reinforce the appearance of levity, fragility and suspension in space. (B2)*

▼ *View of the limit of the façade from the staircase that goes up to the top floor. Wooden furniture is again used on the marble floor and a service door can be made out. (C1)*

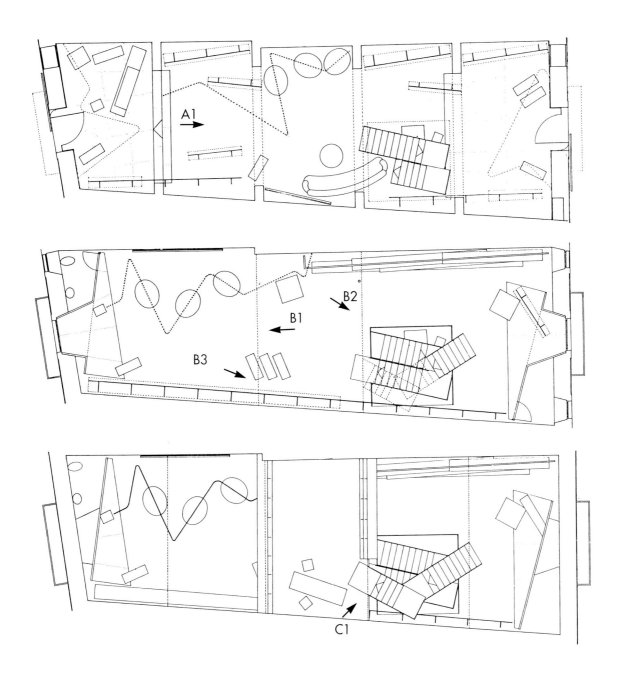

▲ *Ground, middle and top floors. On the ground floor, lines and objects at different angles interplay with the galleries. The façades of the middle floor open out their interior fittings thus introducing new spaces and converting openings into prisms. The office upstairs takes up the central gallery.*

33

▲ *Wood, always of the same tone, is the main trait of the flooring and the furniture. A set of three display pieces which have the appearance of armchairs. (B3)*

◀ *The black sections of the staircase stand out in comparison with the yellow upholstery of the sofa, the wood of the table and the parquet. Next to the sofa, a mirror also has a black frame*

JEAN PIERRE VICTIM'S

Eduard Samsó

The chair, in a modernist style, as one of the pieces of furniture in the shop. The small back contrasts with the length of the legs joined by a metal part that is used as a foot rest.

▶ The design is determined by the gallery in which the shop is located. The space of reduced dimensions opening out onto the passage effectively means that the shop is a shop window. The wooden flooring is the

In 1982, two years after finishing his studies of architecture, Eduard Samsó designed the small shoeshop, Bis de Bis, a subtle, minimalist work, but of a certain importance. It was the beginning of a series of boutiques that would open new horizons in the sector of interior design in Barcelona making Samsó one of its figures of the last decade.

In 1990, at almost the same time as The End was finished on Ibiza, another project by Samsó finished; Jean Pierre Victim's.

The shop forms part of a representative gallery in the city of Barcelona, Boulevard Rosa, located near via Augusta and the Diagonal. The premises could really be described as being a residual space due to its reduced dimensions. It is one of many such premises that make up the interior walkway of the gallery.

Samsó was faced with a difficult space, a space with not much depth and irregularities. The floorspace poses two clear limits; on one hand, a long extension of façade which opens

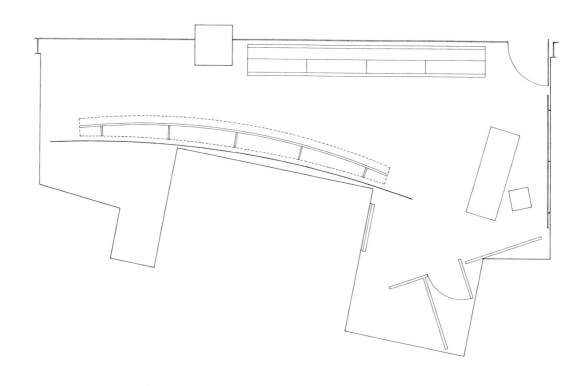

◄ Floor plan. On the edges of the sunken back wall, new fittings have been used to define the corners as service areas as well as unifying the space for the glass façade.

◄ The lighting always acts in function of the products on display and bring out the grey continuity between the walls and ceiling. Fixed to the wall, bare metallic bars show off complements. Next to the counter, stands for ashtrays or for displaying footwear. (B1)

▲ The mannequins lined up next to the shop window establish a subtle difference between the interior and exterior.

onto the passageway, on the other, the back wall falls back with corners and edges.

The chosen solution is clever; available space is made use of, at the same time as creating a new perception of the same by employing fittings that give it a new shape that hide the imperfections.

The first decision was to consider both the shop window and the shop as the same entity. The window is completely glass and is divided into two areas by one of the structural pillars of the building. The bigger area to the left of the pillar contains the entrance at one of its extremes, a mannequin and a display case with three shelves at different angles depending on whether it is displaying merchandise to the exterior or the interior. The smaller part of the window shows mannequins dressed by the most famous fashion designers. Behind the glass window, the space

▲ Two of the shelves of the display
case of the façade slope towards the
interior. In the background, next to the
entrance, a mannequin seems to be
looking out into the passage and is
about to leave. (B2)

becomes a stage. The acts of observing or being observed, buying or selling become actions that are confused and complement each other.

Opposite the entrance supported on one of the edges of the back wall, a marble plane at a slight angle is seen. On one hand it acts as a background for the sales counter, in the ceiling two halogen spotlights are directed at the anagram of the shop in gilt letters on the marble in question. On the other, it distributes the fitting area in a corner behind it.

Another element is a convex wall which is fitted along the length of wall nearest the façade without touching it. The wall continues in front of the other remaining corner turning it into a storeroom. The wall is covered with red velvet that falls in soft folds. A wooden shelf and a metal bar for hangers emphasise the curvature of the wall.

The choice and combination of the materials and colours (the dark red velvet

▲ *Behind the shop window the space appears as a stage. The merchandise is, together with the lighting and furniture, a formal element of the interior design.*

41

▲ The interior of the fitting rooms
is simple and again wood is
predominant; flooring, stool and the
mirror frame. (B3)

curtain and white and grey grained marble fitting) reminds one of the work done for the shop The End. Here as well, wood, although in a darker tone, is the predominant feature of the flooring and the basis of the furniture.

The fittings of marble and velvet reshape the back wall and distribute the space of the shop making use of the corners and acting as a backdrop for the performance.

Another example of the creative ability of Eduard Samsó. ▨

▲ *The counter, an original piece in the same wood as the parquet, has short inclined legs and a glass top.*

▶ *The combination of shadows of the velvet with the wood and metal is added to by the colours and singularity of the products on display.*

▼ *From the interior, there is a change of role; the passage becomes the shop window-stage, window shoppers become mannequins and the other shops become background decoration.*

▲ Velvet and marble, two theatrical fittings that reshape the
depth of the corners and provide a backdrop that
brings out the importance of the firm.

JERRY PAIR

Thompson Ventulett Stainback & Associates

▲ *The space remodelled by Thompson Ventulett Stainback & Associates had to include, as well as the showroom for Jerry Pair and & Associates, another independent space for Jim Thompson Ltd., that is seen in the foreground.*

▶ *Area destined to furniture located behind the sales counter, where lighting can be adapted to changes in the showroom space by means of a set of spotlights on rails attached to the ceiling.*

The renovation of the showroom at the Atlanta Decorative Arts Centre provides a good example of how to organize a showroom of these characteristics by means of a simple but effective distribution scheme which provides a clear layout for the user and takes maximum advantage of available space. In this case, the "spine" of the project is a diagonal walkway which links the main areas thus partitioning the floorspace to allow two types of display.

The use of materials, textures and lighting as resources to delimit areas, signal walkways and to reinforce the importance of the items displayed above the architectural environment, as these are the real "stars" of the showroom.

The firm of architects Thompson, Ventulett, Stainback & Associates of Atlanta, Georgia, have more than 25 years of experience in architecture and interior design. Their set-up of small semi-independent offices has enabled

them to take on a large variety of projects which range from interior design of small premises to large shopping centres. Some of their main projects are the Long Beach Convention Centre, the Omni Arena and Georgia Dome stadiums, the Georgia World Congress Centre and the buildings of the Concourse Complex.

The possibility of renovating the Atlanta Decorative Arts Centre, a showroom destined to furniture, decorative items and home accessories and which belongs to the firm Jerry Pair and Associates, arose when the company which shared the premises, Clarence House, moved its offices to another site within the same complex. TVS&A was commissioned to renovate the 930 m² of showroom, which had not been significantly altered since 1982. The client laid down some very clear prerequisites about the general design of the make-up and running of the showroom; emphasis of the item displayed rather than the surrounding

◀ *View of the rotunda at the end of the main walkway, where the change in flooring is seen from walkways (limestone) to display (carpet), as well as the use of plasterboard ceiling above the boutique. (A2)*

◀ *Starting point of the main walkway from the entrance rotunda, showing the different finishes of the ceiling. The zoning produced by these finishes on the different parts of the shop can be seen.*

▼ *View of the main walkway of the shop from the boutique. The two rotundas at the ends of the walkway are seen and are illuminated by hanging lamps.*

architecture, distribution of areas and walkways which optimize all available space to the maximum and that encourage both easy and pleasant shopping, the setting up of a natural reception area where customers are personally welcomed and reservation of an area where a boutique would be established, the Jim Thompson Thai Silk showroom.

Organisation of space follows a scheme in which the three main components of the showroom; reception, sales counter and the delivery and storage area are linked by means of a slightly off-diagonal walkway from which the layout resembles that of a comb consisting of a series of parallel display wings in which available space is optimized to the maximum. This walkway goes from the entrance and reception area located within a circular rotunda to another rotunda around which are the delivery and storage area and the boutique. The sales counter is located halfway along the main walkway thus enhancing its linearity and

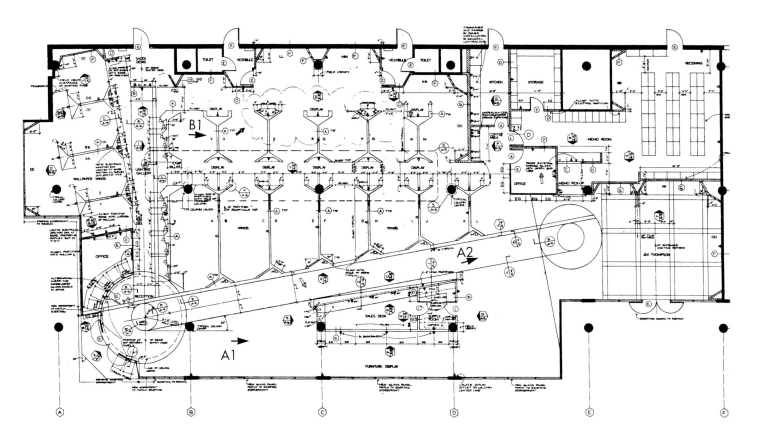

▲ Floor plan.

◄ View of the main walkway from the furniture area where the angle produced by the display wings as they open up towards the entrance create display areas which are visually very attractive.

► View of the main walkway where it meets the end rotunda around which the boutique and delivery and storage areas are located.

▲ Secondary walkway which divides the main display wings bordered by display units at an angle. This walkway is highlighted by the plasterboard ceiling and special overhead lighting. (B1)

► One of the arrangements of lighting, fabric and furniture located at one of the intersections where the wings meet the walkways and are used to promote new products.

creating a visual triangle which relates to the two main areas.

The display areas are located on both sides of the main walkway in a partition of the showroom space which removes the typical back parts of the shop, which do not favour shopping. Within the larger area there are two rows of wings where products such as fabrics, lights and wallpapers are displayed and either lead on to the main walkway, providing a clear view from the sales counter, or to a secondary walkway which also starts from the entrance rotunda. The height of the display wings has been reduced to partly minimize their size and to help ventilation of the premises. Where the walkways and the wings meet, the wings open out in an angle which face towards the entrance and create several small display areas where different arrangements of lights, fabrics and furniture are used to promote new products. The smaller area behind the sales counter is destined to furniture and is an open space which allows great flexibility of display

with a special lighting set-up of spotlights on rails which turns this part of the showroom into a stage where the textures and shapes of furniture may be set off theatrically.

The finishes used on walls, flooring and ceilings possess a neutral colour and texture scheme which show off the displayed products at the same time as helping to mark out areas and show walkways. The limestone flooring used in the main walkway and in the two rotundas together with the carpeting in the display areas as well as the continuous span of black which extends over the displayed products giving way to plasterboard ceilings above the walkways, rotundas and sales counters are changes in decoration which help people find themselves about within the shop. ■

▲ *The sales counter is located on the main walkway opposite the display wings at a central point which provides a direct view of the main areas of the shop.*

GALLERI

Studio Granda

▲ *View of the access to the new space added to the shop, separated by the blue volume of fitting rooms and sales counter opposite it.*

► *The sales counter hides its functional utility with its use as a display item and also through the way it blends in with the wooden flooring. (A2)*

◀ The design of the sales counter makes it a free-standing rectangular form panelled with the same wood as the floor.

▼ The fitting rooms provide a background to the main sales counter, both are independent items in the decor, which contribute to the centralised layout with the products displayed on shelves or rails on the surrounding walls.

The enlargement of the fashion shop, Eva-Galleri, provides a clear example of how to structure a project by means of a simple, but effective strategy. In this case, it is the placing of a set of free-standing fitting rooms, separated from the peripheral walls, that functionally and spatially organises the premises due to its central position and to the special finish of its surface, which turns it into a visual and organisational focal point. Around the structure, the subtle use of fittings and materials and the distribution of the products along the walls further augments its central position.

Studio Granda in Iceland is made up of the young architects, Margret Hardardottir (Reykjavik,1959) and Steve Christer (Blackfyne, United Kingdom, 1960). After their studies in architecture in Great Britain, they set up their studio in 1987 in Reyjavik. In their short career, projects such as Reykjavik Town Hall

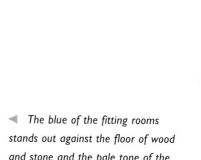

◀ The blue of the fitting rooms stands out against the floor of wood and stone and the pale tone of the surrounding walls and ceiling.

*General view from the entrance
to the shop, where the change in the
flooring, from wood to stone,
is seen. (A1)*

(1992) and the dwellings in Wiesbaden (Germany, 1992) stand out, where they show their concern for combining natural, cultural and functional factors to make the architectural process appear as a result of natural development.

The young people's fashion shop "Galleri" is located in the same building as the boutique "Eva" and the life-style shop "Company" and both belong to the same company, Eva h.f. The project by Studio Ganda enlarges this shop by using an old office located between the existing shop and "Eva". The original premises, a rectangle of approximately 12.5 x 4 metres with three exterior facades, is increased by a small area of 4.5 x 3 metres which makes a T shape. The connection between the two is effected by a doorway in the wall.

A prismatic volume that reaches the ceiling and contains two fitting rooms, situated between the two rectangles that make up the floorspace is where the new item organises the space due to its central position. The siting of the customer attention counter, to which the fitting rooms act as a background, also contributes to the centralised layout with the products displayed on shelves and rails on the surrounding walls. Access to the premises from one of the corners of the larger rectangle emphasises the influence of the blue prism on the interior.

The use of a dark blue tone for this free-standing body makes it stand out in comparison with the white tones of the ceiling and walls and the flooring of wood and stone. The continuity of the walls is broken by recesses and changes of plane that are made evident by changes on the floor from wood to stone. A continuous mirror in the new part also adds contrast together with the siting of a third fitting room.

The flooring is continuous in all of the premises, but splits into two materials at the fitting rooms. Most of the old shop is floored

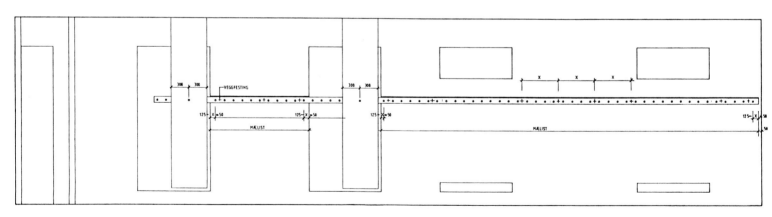

◄ *Longitudinal section of the space towards the façade out on the street.*

with maple panels, while the new shop and part of the old is made up of basalt stone.

The sales counter blends in with the wooden flooring. Its design, which hides away its functional use, makes it seem a special display item. The display fittings on the walls make use of wood and black steel on the pale background and the outside windows.

The lighting of the premises is based on a network of lights sunk into the ceiling augmented by lights fitted on some of the shelves. The existing windows provide natural light, while they have been modified in some cases depending on the needs of the project, though keeping their external appearance. ▨

▼ *Longitudinal section of the space towards the fitting rooms.*

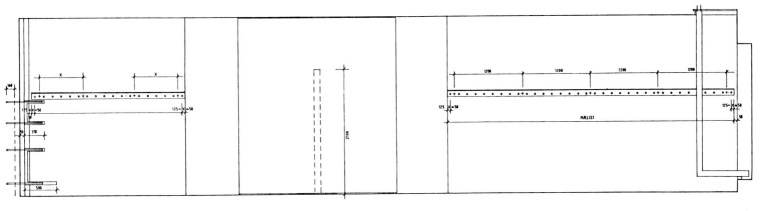

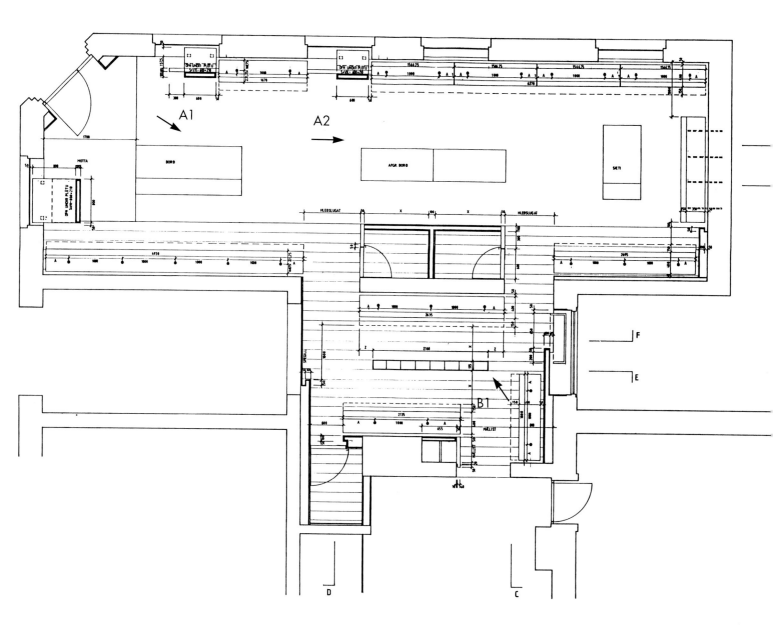

▲ *Floorplan.*

► *In the new part a large mirror has been added. In the background, a partially covered window —which acts as a backdrop to a wooden display case— is reflected. (B1)*

EVA

Studio Granda

▲ The new space which links the Eva and Company shops, located at the end of a court, becomes a centre of visual attraction from the street due to the glass opening which acts as a shop window at street level.

▶ The new wall loses height as it goes into the interior and becomes level with the glass opening to create a passageway where steps overcome the change in level. (B1)

◀ The direction of the new wall which spans the space between the two premises comes from continuing the line of trees which separates the two levels of the exterior space.

▼ Transversal section of the new building. The longitudinal section crosses the court.

▶ The new building is located at the end of a court paved with different sized pieces of granite that gently slope down and seem to penetrate the interior. (A1)

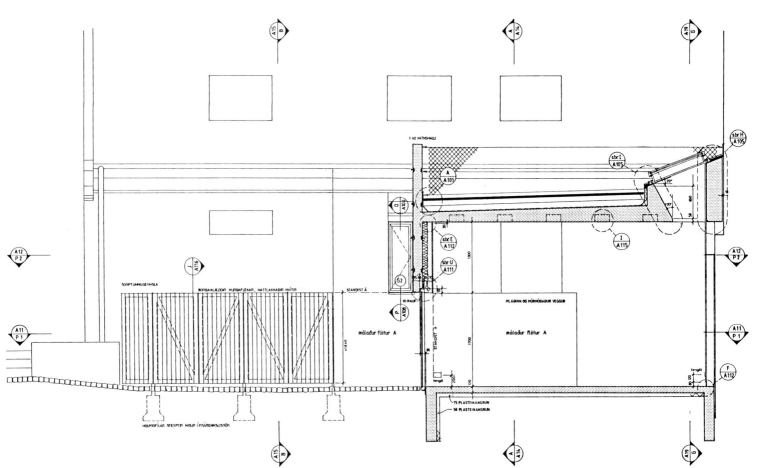

The presence of two fashion premises belonging to the same company on both sides of an external court linked to a street means that the construction of a volume between them can be tackled more ambitiously than simply interconnecting the two shops.

Studio Granda was founded by Margret Haròardóttir (Reykjavik,1959) and Steve Christer (Blackfyne, United Kingdom, 1960) in 1987 and meant the appearance of one of the most promising architectural studios in Iceland. Their main projects, such as the Reyjavik Town Hall (1992) and the dwellings in Wiesbaden (Germany, 1992) are characterised by a special sensibility towards encompassing natural forces of the site, culture, function and time in the architectural work, within which they assign a role of equal importance to the design process as well as construction.

The project was planned as the filling of a

vacuum between two buildings located at the ends of a private court perpendicular to the main access road. The two shops belong to the same company. The siting of the two shops yields the possibility of linking the two premises by means of a common space while setting up a new emporium at the same time.

The new building takes up the end of the space between the walls of the existing buildings and results in a rectangular area of size 5.5 x 9.5 metres with a single façade which takes up half of one of its longer sides. The structure of small pillars is laid out independently of the existing walls, one new wall has been added and is the continuation of the line drawn by the change of level between the new court and the garden at the entrance of the shop "Company" and by a row of trees. The new wall, which starts off being as high as the existing wall next to it, decreases to half this size in the interior. The wall is cleverly positioned without causing impact on its surroundings, at the same time as creating an

◄ *The concrete front of the façade blends in with the white side wall of the existing building.*

◄ *The white wall crowned with a small logo of the shop"Company" seems to come forward to form the space that links the two buildings.*

▼ *Floor plan of the new building.*

interior passageway in which only a few steps show the change of level between the two premises and is the only element that breaks the smoothness of the interior, an almost empty rectangular container with entrances at its ends.

As a result of this layout, the exterior court between the buildings becomes shorter, although it seems to extend further than the glass front into the interior. The floor is made up of pieces of granite of different sizes and the smooth slope towards the building gives way to the polished cement floor of the interior. The fact that the glass front finishes below eye level adds to this effect of continuity which projects the interior space towards the outside.

The façade onto the court is made up of two planes characterized by the simplicity of their materials, an upper plane of cement seems to lie on the white side wall which blends in with the building next door and a continuous glass plane.

The interior space which results is a space of austere shapes, materials and colours, where

B2

B1

A1

67

the items on display seem to have priority and stand out against their surroundings. The layout of the objects in the shop is planned as being peripheral, where they are displayed on the wall. The polished concrete floor and the concrete sandblasted ceiling form two horizontal planes between which the walls in a grey-white tone provide a neutral background.

The natural lighting of the interior is provided by the glass opening in the façade and by the covered skylights over the only wall without openings. Artificial lighting was planned as a uniform layout of lights sunk into the ceiling in an attempt to lighten the mass of the concrete ceiling. ■

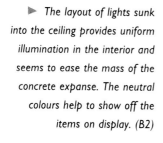 *The austere interior space is defined by the plain greys of the cement ceiling and floor. The walls in grey-white act as a backgound for the fittings in black steel.*

▶ *The layout of lights sunk into the ceiling provides uniform illumination in the interior and seems to ease the mass of the concrete expanse. The neutral colours help to show off the items on display. (B2)*

68

▲ *Artificial lighting in the ceiling*
combines with natural light from the
skylights along the wall
opposite the façade.

ONE STUDIO OFF

Ron Arad

▲ *Details of one of the sculptures of the façade.*

Some of the sculptures of sharp contours which are found in the attic of the building. (B2)

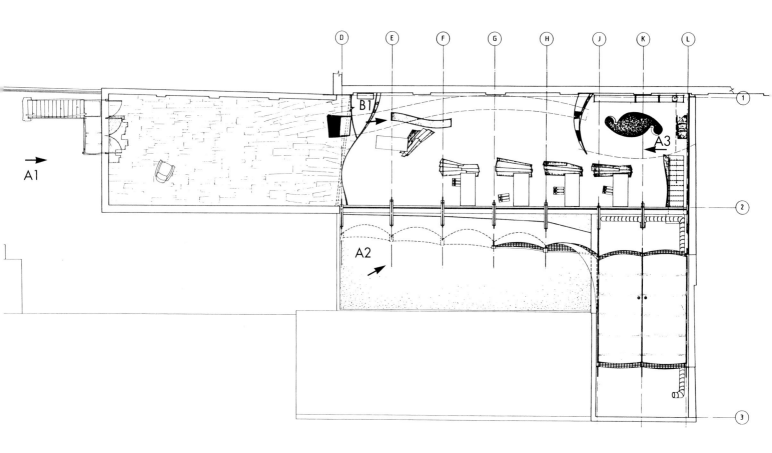

◀ *The exterior brick walls have been painted in an intense blue.*

A few years ago in London a few art and architecture students produced a series of objects which, in the shape of furniture, appeared in the art world. Tables, chairs, shelves had been created from scrap. Rubbish, scrap and rag markets provided the raw material. Each piece therefore depended on a find.

Among these designers, the one that received the greatest recognition was Ron Arad from Israel (Tel Aviv, 1951) who came to London in 1973 and studied until 1979 at the Architectural Association-School of Architecture.

If, at the beginning of the eighties, he formed part of the group of designers in the search for objects that could be re-used, his professional career has taken him along different paths.

For example, the difference between the Rover Chair, a reclining armchair, formed by a tubular structure that supports a car seat and the series of chairs, Eight by One, in which the structure is reduced to the basic elements consisting of an 8-by-1ft sheet of folded steel

◀ *General floor plan.* ▼ *Floor plan of the upper floor.*

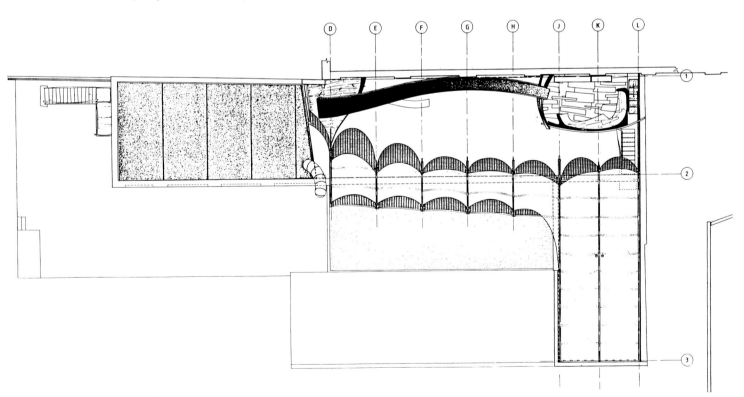

that comprises the back, seat and legs of the chair.

Although his first inclinations tended towards the practice of architecture, in 1981 he founded, together with Dennis Groves and Caroline Thorman, the well-known shop or workshop, One Off. One Off is a place of work, exhibition and sale of furniture in what was previously a fruit store in Covent Garden. What at the beginning was a rundown premises or a meeting place for unsettled young people became the workshop of one of the main designers on the world scene.

Ron Arad presented numerous personal or group exhibitions and in 1986 presented pieces which were to give him his fame as a rebel on the design scene; Horns collection, Shadow of Time, Concrete Stereo, Honeycomb Range, or Well Tempered Chair. He also exhibited in Japan and Germany at that time. On seeing the

outlandish objects created by Arad, some critics described him as a troglodithic futurist, a re-cycler of the post-atomic era, a "Mad Max" style designer. He will be the enfant terrible who, in the Pompidou Centre of Paris, will show a machine that smashes up old chairs that visitors can bring along.

Arad has designed pieces that have quickly become authentic events, such as School Chair for Vitra (1987), the Volumes Collection

▲ *The roof, supported by the decorated pillars, makes clear the change that has taken place in the building.*

▲ *In the foreground, a chair of
the series Eight by One has a
spectacular effect.*

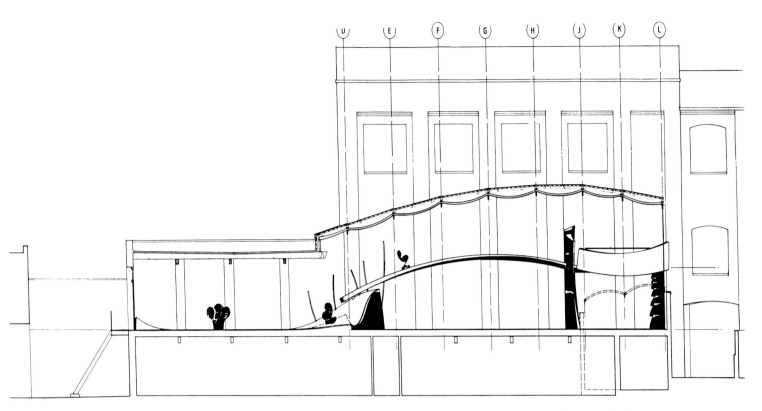

▲ *Longitudinal section.*

(1988) or the Schizo Chair for Vitra Edition that has different formats; one can be fitted into the other or can be split and also changed into a bench. Other works include the Split Table and Chair for Poltronova (1989) or the setting-up of a workshop in the Vitra Design Museum together with Rachel Reynolds and Shaun Crown (1990-1991).

Arad's work is situated between sculpture and design, it is an experiment on the limit of what is needed when an object is designed to be used. It is a question of comfortable furniture, although one does not sit on a conventional chair. For example, in the case of the Well Tempered Chair, a chair with a fragile appearance, made of metal that bends to the limit when it is sat on, as if it were going to break. The objects designed by Ron Arad provide numerous sensations. The sensations arise from the deformation of a type, from the reinterpretation of traditional

design themes; chair, table, shelves, lamp. there is always, in each object, something new that comes from the conflict between the properties of each material and the concept that needs to be developed.

Ron Arad's architectural and design studio was brought together in 1989 in the same premises, the workshop and showroom, One Off. An old building was chosen in the north-east of London, which was painted blue on the outside. In the rundown premises, fifty metres long by five wide, furniture was produced at the same time as it was designed. The result is a physical metaphor of the creative process of the studio, in which there is continuity between the design table and the workbench. There is no separation between the project and manufacture of the product. The architecture of the premises also reflects the same relationship with the objects produced there.

The design of the premises has allowed Ron Arad to experiment with each element of the project; the relief of the floor, the metal roof and the transparent PVC and polyester tarpaulin, light, sinuous, like a skin that is being stretched, the bridge, the smooth windows and the decoration of the pillars. With the aim of creating a division between the furniture showroom and the design area without building a dividing wall, the possibilities of the floor were used. At a certain point the flooring, made up of irregular wooden pieces, starts to rise, like a hill, from where the design area can be observed. From the upper part a narrow

▶ *Detail in section of the roof and of the decorated pillars. (A3)*

▼ *On the following page, the translucent roof provides variation in the light.*

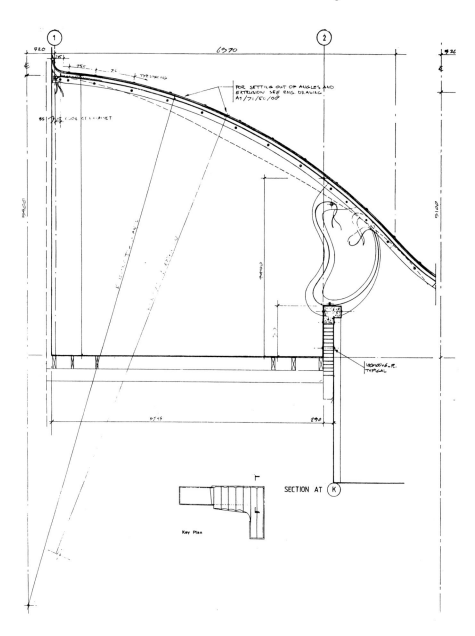

blue bridge leads to an upper floor on which an office is hidden by a panel. The bridge has been installed in situ and is made of steel (10 by 3mm) in such a way that it has a hollow section that can distribute either hot or cold air to different parts of the studio from the air conditioning located under the "hill".

The decorated pillars were to be and were to be the frames for the windows so that they could open with a radius of one metre. However, another solution was chosen, after trying different types of semi-rigid perspex, 8 mm PVC was chosen held by a metal frame. This produced a flexible window that can be opened to any position and fixed following the structure of the pillars. The main function of these structures is to provide a support for the roof using triangular fittings. The initials of the studio, One Off are seen in the decoration of the pillars. ▪

◀ *The air-conditioning bridge also provides a base for a series of furniture. (B1)*

▼ *From the "hill" the design area is seen below.*

DOLCE & GABBANA (Uomo)

Claudio Nardi

▲ *Between the deep ceiling and and the worked floor, the smooth surface of the walls supports simple glass shelves.*

▷ *Completely open to the street, the space is a result of surface, spatial and illumination work within a simple container. In the top part of the façade, two spotlights point to the interior. (A1)*

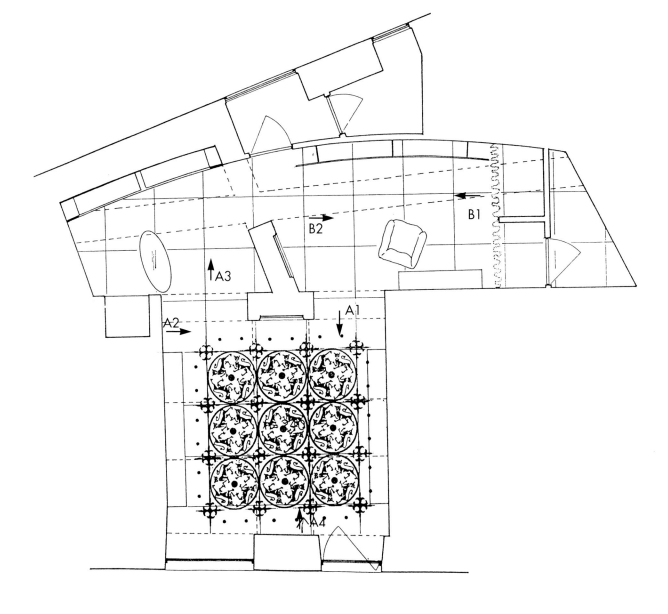

When an architect receives a commission on behalf of an important company in the world of fashion for designing one of its shops, the design may turn into a question of image. Even more so if the shop is located in Milan, the city of fashion and Italian design. It should be hoped that its interior will reflect the image of the company in accordance with its products and clearly indentify with its target group of customers.

The architect must take into account these facts when planning out the space. Claudio Nardi from Florence is the creator of the men's wear shop, Dolce & Gabbana, located at number 10 Via Sant'Andrea in Milan. For Nardi, the creative architectural idea comes from the space with which he has to work, as well as the reasons behind the commission.

The Via Sant'Andrea is a pedestrian street in which various businesses are located. The new shop takes up the ground floor of one of the buildings.

The façade, with a thick central section, has two glass openings at its extremes. The entrance to the shop, at the extreme right, leads through to a square gallery. The floor of all of the shop has been covered with dark grey slate tiles, but it is in this space where the decoration of the shop reaches its greatest splendour with a motif of lions and flowers painted on the floor. The drawing has been done by hand following an ancient tradition which still exists in Florence to this day.

This initial space provides majestic serenity. On its bare side walls glass shelves and a metal bar for hangers are seen. Opposite the façade, the intermediate wall repeats the decoration of

◀ *Floor plan and a simulated axonometric perspective. From the square gallery to the spaces shaped by the curvature of the back wall. A door in the wall leads through to the storeroom.*

▶ *Behind the collector's item is the oval counter, a functional item of glass and metal. In the background, the white wall contains fitted shelves. (A3)*

▽ *Contrast in harmony. The bareness of the fittings brings together the ornamental woodwork of the furniture and the sculpted plasterwork of the floor with the subtle clarity of the glass shelves. (A2)*

the side walls, while the decor provides the base for a piece of furniture, a Louis XV-style sofa with red velvet upholstery, hand finished in gilt wood.

In an attempt to furnish a certain style to the space, the walls and ceiling have been furbished in the same plasterwork painted in oxide. The result is an interior of ochre and of a sculptural character. Especially the ceiling, the corners of which seem to have been carved out to form a structure in the shape of a cross.

Nardi sculpts the decor of a container which he has been given and in the interior space, he gathers objets d'art and traditions of his birthplace, as well as simple lines of modern materials for the display and sale of fashion designs. A balance of contrasts within an essentially classical environment.

Through the back doorways, a white curved wall is seen at the back which runs parallel to

85

▲ Apart from its use as a support for the sofa, the intermediate wall stabilizes the space of the square room. Its presence contrasts with the white background of the back wall, which displays new products. (A4)

▶ The sales area at the back of the shop introduces white in the shape of the curved wall. The space is defined by the surface continuity of the curve and is reflected by the framed mirror of the angled wall and offers fragmented perspectives which invite movement. (B1)

86

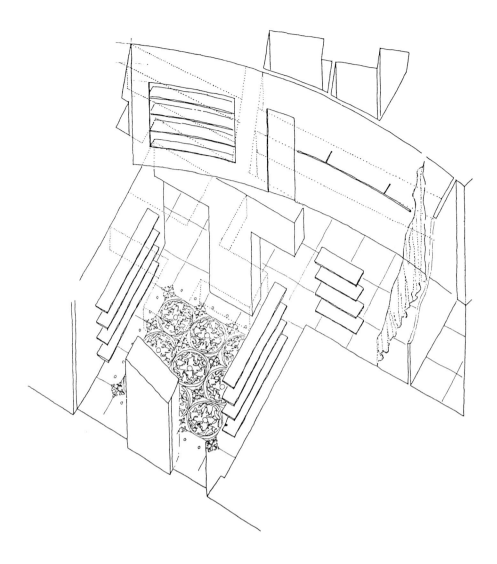

the street and which unifies the back spaces of
the shop. Both doorways lead through to sales
areas in which the curved wall displays its
products in an uncustomary way, on the side
facing the fitting rooms, a bar for hangers is
seen, while on the the side of the counter, the
wall has been hollowed out into which glass-
doored cupboards have been installed.

After the classical decor of the first gallery,
the visitor finds walls at an angle to the
flooring decor with furniture that is also at an
angle to the corners. The contrast is also
seen in the space which is now irregular
and dynamic.

Back in the street, the roof attracts
attention. Within the confines of this shop,
Dolce & Gabbana obtain the seal which
identifies it among the many clothes businesses
in Milan. ■

▲ *Axonometric projection*
of the premises.

▶ *Combination of colours*
and materials at the entrance of
the fitting rooms. The hardness
and durability which are
characteristic of slate are found
throughout the shop. (B2)

DOLCE & GABBANA (Donna)

Claudio Nardi

▲ The glass opening of the façade is conceived as a shop window for an image. The originality of the pieces, their careful manufacture and the memory of the past are ideas which are in harmony with the personality of Dolce & Gabbana.

▶ The trapezoidal shape of the white carpet complements the decoration of the slate tiles and perfectly fits the recess of the façade. It provides a perfect base for the display of the chaise longue. (A1)

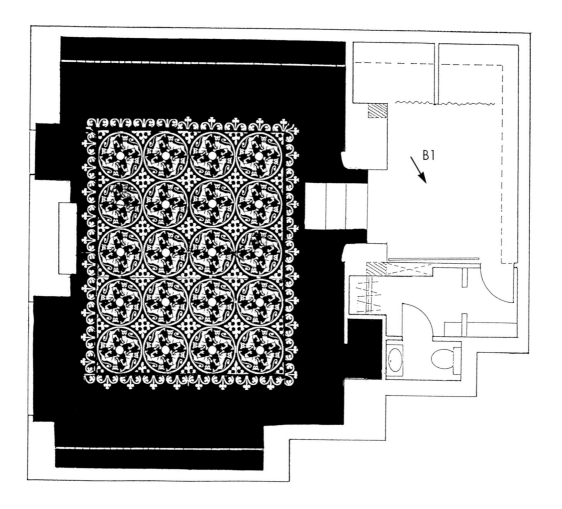

A short time after history repeats itself;
the same company, the same city and the
same architect.

Situated in la Via della Spiga, the shop,
Dolce & Gabbana Donna, follows the same
lines as the men's wear shop. The same motif
in a different space. This time the ground floor
has a longer façade and the area of the surface
of the premises could be defined as a rectangle
that falls back into one of its corners.

The façade, characterised by green, has two
framed openings; the entrance door and a
large window that almost reaches the
pavement. A quick look on the part of a
passer-by in a hurry will take in the interior of
an aristocratic room, from another time.
Behind the glass of the shop window, a white
chaise longue of imperial times poses

slightly inclined. To the right an illuminated
opening in the wall reminds one of the warmth
of a fireside and, at the back, a decorated
table is seen.

The conventional concept of a shop window
loses all meaning in the Dolce & Gabbana shops
designed by Claudio Nardi. The openings in the
façade do not display designs by the company,
but act as shop windows for the interior space
and image of the firm. Along the same lines, the
piece of furniture that appears in the shop
window is not functional, but something that
symbolizes the personality of Dolce & Gabbana.

The entrance leads directly through to a
rectangular room, that is almost square and
that repeats the sculpted plasterwork on the
slate floor and the ochre finish on walls and
ceiling. As in the case of the men's wear shop,

◀ Between the two illuminated openings, an antique table equips the corner space and converses with the clothes.

◀ Floor plan and partial axonometry. A simple composition of orthogonal surfaces; the main room, the fitting rooms and the service rooms.

▶ Modern clothes, shoes and other accessories rest on glass shelves or on metal bars. The lighting sets off the colour of the products and plays with the texture and depth of the walls.

◀ Detail of the ochre tones of the walls.

93

the curved wall again reappears as fundamental in the definition of the sales area. While the ceiling remains flat, the walls acquire depth. The decor of the façade or the use of panels on the side walls produce the same effect of body and depth as that of the ceiling in the men's wear shop. The only difference being that as they are vertical fittings they fulfil the role normally played by furniture. The relief they provide supplies places for transparent shelves and bars for hanging clothes. The sculptural concept becomes functional.

The plasterwork on the slate tiles forms a central seal in the room, which bounds its space. To the right of the entrance, two pieces of furniture are placed at an angle at the corners of the floor decoration as a contrast to its stability. The table is the same style as the sofa in the men's wear shop with details in gilt wood. Its location in the corner turns it into the counter space. On the other hand, the chaise longue rests on a specially

▲   *The relationship with the exterior is simple and direct. On the inside surface of the façade, large spotlights set the scene for the interior. (A2)*

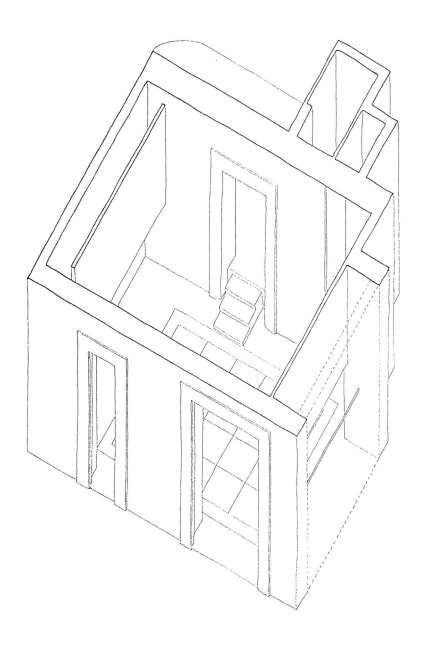

▲ *Partial axonometric projection.*

▲ The finish of the walls and ceiling
provides a setting that links pieces,
textures, materials and different colours
to form a selective interior.

▶ The frame of the entrance to the
fitting rooms contrasts and stands out
for its purity, both in terms of
shape and colour. (A3)

designed white carpet making it a work of art for display.

On the intermediate wall, a large white frame marks out the back of the shop, at a slightly different level to the rest. A step, also in white, provides access to the back part. In this area the customers can try on clothes and look at themselves. It is a complementary space with a great poetic force, decorated in white with a mirror and multicoloured curtains. The fitting rooms are to the left behind the curtains and the white frame of the mirror takes up the right wall. A concealed door at the back leads through to a small storeroom and washroom.

A shop with two areas, two different spaces, both of which static, with the same sensibility. ■

▼ *Detail of the ornate shelves set into the interior of the façade. The concept is always the same; the use of the recesses in the wall as display space.*

◄ *Reflected in the mirror, a white room with curtains, coloured rug and a traditional plain wooden seat in the corner. (B1)*

SAN FRANCISCO STORY

Claudio Nardi

▲ *Between the arches of the ancient façade of the building, a discrete metal plate has been fitted. Behind, the interior of the shop is framed and lit like a stage.*

▶ *The transition space between the street and the shop window seems to look like the entrance of a house with a garden outside. A cosy space that draws attention.*

◀ *Different hand-drawn perspectives of the interior space. The staircase that goes round a pillar leading to the basement appears in all of them.*

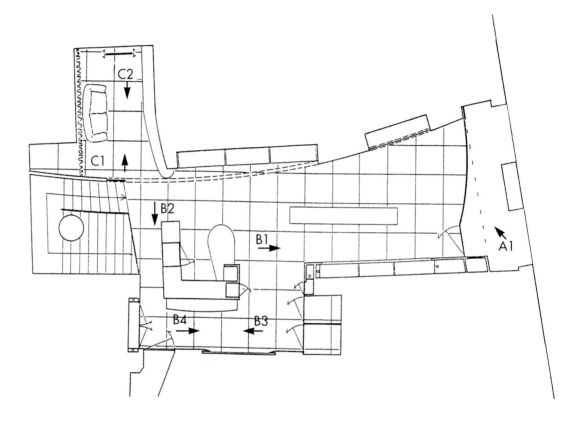

▲ *The floor plan shows the work carried out on the perimeter walls and the layout of the shop by means of two central structures.*

▶ *The position of the mirror directly on the floor produces optical illusions of spatial depth and amplitude.*

During the same period as the Dolce & Gabbana shops, the shop, San Francisco Story, was commissioned by a Japanese promoter that teamed up the Florence architect, Claudio Nardi with his birthplace, with the aim of creating a commercial atmosphere which would be identified with American fashion of the 1930's. The intention was to define a corporative image that would also be used, in the not too distant future, in other shops that the company plans to open in different parts of the world.

The premises is located at number 77/79 in the busy Via Porta Rossa. The façade of this ancient building is dominated by the symmetry of two arches and a small central pediment. Nardi inserts a transition area between the street and the entrance to the shop. The arches look like cutouts in the old façade and are glazed at the back in the upper part and have gates in the lower part. During the day, when the shop is open, the gates of horizontal black bars are folded up into the side walls.

After this short trip into the past, the space opens into the interior of the shop through a large copper oxide frame. The frame, lit from the ceiling by a row of spotlights, seems to be a stage in which the large oval mirror of the shop window leads one into. The main element of the shop window is a panel with a black and white photograph of the emblematic Golden Gate bridge.

▲ *The use of reflections and translucence in the area between the entrance and the fitting rooms. The wooden flooring offers quality versus the marble in the rest of the shop.*

▶ *The overhead lighting, the oval mirror and the seating area characterise one of the sales areas.*

The existing space is the starting point. The floorspace, which is somewhat irregular, can be considered as longitudinal and narrows from the façade to open out on the left and in the right-hand corner and finishes at a stairway.

The floor is tiled with dark grey Levantine marble tiles. The ceiling and most of the walls are plastered in white. A few glass shelves and bars for hanging clothes are incrusted in the surface of the walls, others are found in the

▲ *The stairs at the back go round a thick white pillar. The handrail, of thick metallic bars, is fixed to it.*

luminous white of its recesses. Between the walls the layout of the furniture aids movement within the shop.

From the entrance a long glass display case with a wooden interior and steel structure together with three spherical lamps suspended from the ceiling suggests the first movements through space. The cherry wood panelling of the side wall that continues to other walls or the furniture layout also guides movement through the shop. To the left, the wood covers the lintel of the entrance and is used for shelves on the walls.

The space continues to the remaining sectors and again well-lit display cases and glass shelves are seen on the white walls as well as reflections in mirrors, the translucence of the doors of the fitting rooms or a pair of armchairs with curtains in the background.

In the background stairs descend to the lower floor of the shop....

The projects of Claudio Nardi seem to reflect on how the walls of a shop have to be, especially when the space is difficult and good use needs to be made of it. On this occasion, the walls function as furniture, or is it a case of the opposite? ■

▲ *The walkway that leads to the staircase a predominance of simplicity of detail is seen.*

◄ *Detail of the opening that, apart from showing accessories using glass shelves and internal lighting, allows visual communication between the two sides of the wall.*

▲ The illuminated display case focuses one of the areas of movement, in which the white of the walls and the transparency of glass predominate.

► The vertical fittings accompany the flow of the whole space and define smaller spaces for display. Their depth makes this possible.

► The combination of metal, wood and glass forms display cases both in the shape of furniture or on the walls. The white backlighting of the shelves shows off the objects on display.

TEMPUS

FRCH Design Worldwide

▲ *The glass front shows the sales pull; an attractive interior world filled with colour and rich detail. Two classical items are seen here; a sculpture and a column.*

▶ *The giant sculpture seems to have left its pedestal to run through the glass front into the interior.*

Within the midst of a public thoroughfare, the Mall of America in the city of Bloomington, the Tempus Entertainment group decided to open a new establishment. Its primary function is not only to entertain, but also to educate (somehow) and, of course, to sell.

The impact factor of the building seems to have been borrowed from the most up-to-date theme parks. Inside, people can experience the latest in virtual reality with high-definition digital images, electronic simulation of movement and dramatic special effects.

Leisure culture is getting modern!

The project, considered to be a prototype, is the work of the Cincinnati office of FRCH Design Worldwide (formally SDI-HTI). Behind the letters FRCH are more than 200 design professionals who work in different areas; architecture, interior design, graphic design, lighting, visual marketing and construction services. It may be said that projects for commercial establishments such as Tempus, in which the visual identity (from the logo to carrier bags) needs to be created, is the speciality of this particular company. The process starts with a strategy, almost marketing

▲ Above the entrance, the gearwheels of an enormous mechanism hang. The same theme is also seen in the drawing on the floor.

◀ View of the space that leads to the simulation cabins which are to the right. In the darkness of the atmosphere, projections and light beams from spotlights stand out. Other light points are set on circular platforms hanging from the ceiling.

▶ One of the sales points with a vast range of items is laid out around a statue. The statue in question is the Venus de Milo complete with mechanical arms.

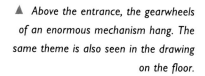

in character, whose aim is an effective design that identifies the position of the client with the needs of its consumers.

The sales area is located next to the walkway to catch the eye of passers-by and also acts as an unavoidable filter for whoever would like to have a go on one of the side-shows, located at the end of the site. Tempus makes its guests undergo a series of hair-raising adventures which chronologically narrate mankind's ingenuity, emphasizing its achievements. These stories are thematically related with the design of the establishment and the extraordinary selection of merchandise on sale.

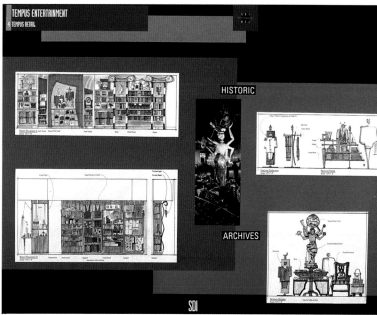

▲ *Images and different studies of various display fittings. Note the classical reference and the combination of colours.*

◄ *On the previous page, another of the sales points with lamps that hang from the ceiling and a violet floor carpeted with letters and numbers.*

◄ *Colour perspective of a previous version of the façade with two columns.*

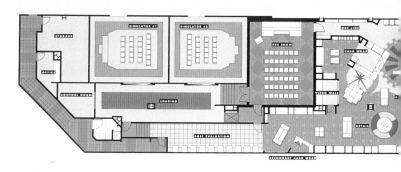

▶ *General floor plan of the project with coloured flooring. The different focal points of the space devoted to sales separate the street from the quieter area containing the cabins.*

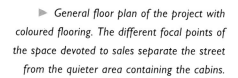

◄ *Tempus Expeditions also sells its own line of products. Here the logo is seen on a sweatshirt, it is also used on its labels.*

▼ *Logo and sign of the Tempus Entertainment group. The sign is a flat design in which the "e" acquires a certain importance. The logo offers a three-dimensional design in which the same "e" starts as the shadow of the "T".*

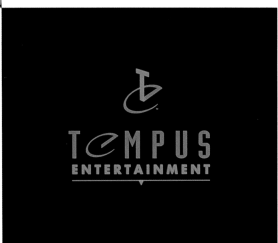

The design brings to life, with a lot of imagination, the great achievements of humanity. The first details of this appear at the entrance divided into three glass sections.

A robust classical sculpture of a sun-bronzed nude body goes from the entrance to the interior, penetrating the left-hand part. An extract from a scene of the comedy, As You Like It, by William Shakespeare, can be seen on the curved glass.

The entrance is made up of the central section below the red neon sign. It is flanked by a grotesque column decorated with parts of a clock and other mechanisms on the wood and on which busts of famous personalities from history are seen on the capital, such as Leonardo da Vinci or Christopher Columbus.

Above the entrance an enormous set of cogwheels hanging from the ceiling represents human invention. The drawing on the floor, centred at the column, repeats the image of a gear wheel. An image that constantly appears

◀ *Shelves filled with articles. Once again classical designs are seen, this time in the shape of volutes as decorative items.*

and symbolizes the wheels of time.

The sales area is located to the left of the entrance. It is an area that is decorated with coloured shelves full of articles, a few items of classical art and a patterned carpet of letters and numbers on a violet background.

Opposite, a giant video screen shows parts of the latest side-show. Towards the right, the sales counter is located in front of two imposing arches which represent architectural feats. Behind, there is the direct access to the first conventional hall with seating for 42 people in which the visitors can see a preliminary adventure film of what they are about to experience. After, they continue along a lengthy illuminated space which leads to the two simulation cabins with seating for 21 people.

Similar simulators have a hydraulic system for each seat. However, Tempus uses an electrical simulator which causes movement in the whole cabin. A mechanism with six degrees of movement provides a breathtaking experience for customers.

The circuit is completed with a wide walkway to which a series of video monitors shows visitors the thrills they have experienced. This area leads back to the sales area in which visitors have another opportunity to see the merchandise on display.

When this prototype in the Mall of America in the city of Bloomington (Minnesota) has been fully tested, Tempus plans to distribute the concept to shopping centres throughout the country. A new combination for sales, entertainment and an ironic look at the history of mankind. ▪

▼ *Video monitor area in which the visitors can relive the experiences they have undergone. The varied decoration also provides amusement.*

GREAT MALL

FRCH Design Worldwide

▲ The boat court uses nautical features in recreating the deck of a transatlantic liner. Details, such as the air vents, are used to house video monitors.

▶ View of the entrance tower to one of the courts. The metal structure shows the entrance and the thematic image is outlined using neon lights.

◀ *Exterior of the car plant with the parking forecourt in the foreground and the hills in the background. Some signs and mainly the structures at the entrances show the new use of the factory.*

▼ *Gas station borders around old gas pumps and original Coca-Cola dispensing machines, seats from racing cars, lamp-posts and traffic lights. At the top, three panels or dioramas in movement represent the Californian landscape.*

When an immense car manufacturing plant, such as that of Ford in Milpitas (California), becomes vacant, the potential of its vast interior space is revealed. The space is the same, but different. The absence of activity cleanses it and leaves it naked. A space that remembers its past while waiting, immutable, for change.

The team that represents FRCH Design Worldwide in Cincinnati was commissioned to provide a new use to the building that was projected by Wah Yee Associates. The aim was to turn the factory into a new shopping centre, to create a pleasant, entertaining centre which would be convenient for shopping. A project, a priori, of an interior design character, but with exterior connotations.

The shopping centre is laid out following a thematic walkway in the shape of a ring. Along the walkway, five special points are located in the shape of a court. Each one of them has a direct entrance that links it with the exterior. The design of the courts shows different means of transport in bygone times, paying homage to the previous activity of the factory. The courts are the following; cars of the fifties, boats of the thirties, trains of 1890, planes of the sixties and a final court that summarises the above themes about travel; the food court.

Access to the courts is by entrance towers added to the façade. They are used as orientation points and show images of what is

◀ *A large sculpted prow receives*
visitors in the boat court. The ceramic
flooring marks out the rest of the ship.

▼ *In the car court, an old Ford model*
that was made in the factory is shown
under the skylights and metallic
structure of the roof.

to be found inside; a Ford of the fifties
speeding along a road, a steamship entering the
Bay of San Francisco, an old train on the tracks
at Milpitas or an aeroplane rising into the sky.

In the interior, each court forms an
integrally designed (or decorated) theme. The
shopfronts, the sales kiosks, the flooring, the
seating areas, the lighting, the decor....,
everything, absolutely everything, aims to
recreate situations and the atmosphere of
bygone times in an effort to amaze the visitor.

In the centre of the car court, for example, a restored Ford, an original from the production line of this particular factory, revolves on a rotating platform. Every 15 minutes the roof rises and folds up in the boot to again return to its original position. The sales kiosks recreate a period gas station or the front of a motel of the fifties. On the ground, motorway markings are seen or yellow borders forming islands, the seats are from

▲ *The star of the aeroplane court is a brilliant chassis of a four-motor plane. Suspended from the roof, it moves through a sky complete with clouds.*

▼ *Some of the sales kiosks. The original roof lets light through the structure and skylights, providing the same atmosphere in all of the courts.*

◀ *General plan of the shopping centre in which the route around the different courts is seen, as well as the shop areas and other service areas.*

racing cars and the shopfronts are decorated with traffic lights.....

Similar set-ups can be seen in the other courts. The different dioramas make up routes showing different scenes related with the history of transport. All of the scenes are below the same roof, a diaphanous roof of translucent skylights and metallic girders.

The focal point in the boat court is the pool (together with a fountain) from the deck of a transatlantic liner. This time the kiosks recreate lighthouses or a cabin next to a palm. If the fountain is turned off, the pool can be covered and used as a stage for shows or special events.

If the four thematic courts function as meeting and rest points, the shopping centre also offers the Great Food Court; a large area of tables surrounded by fast food establishments. A nice detail when thinking about spending the whole day in the Great Mall of the Bay Area. ■

▲ *A group of Victorian-style sofas and armchairs on a flowered carpet recalls the style of the first-class journeys by train at the beginnings of the century.*

◀ *Under the diaphanous roof, the Great Food Court is a large space full of tables, surrounded by counters of fast food. A necessary space for large shopping centres that manage to entertain their visitors during all of the day.*

121

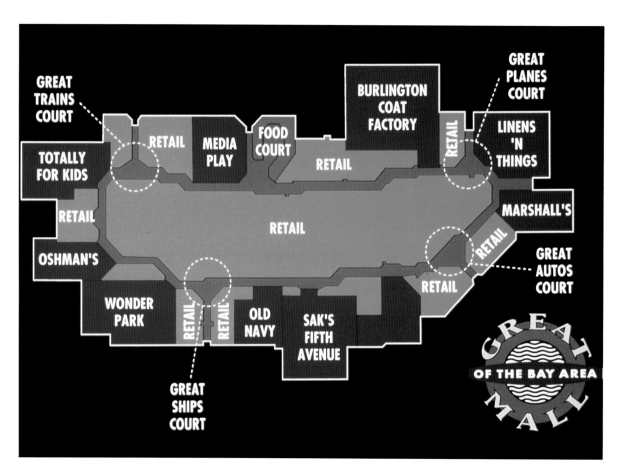

◀ *General plan of the shopping centre
in which the itinerary around the
different courts, as well as the shopping
and other areas is seen.*

◀ ▼ *Next to the palms, tables with collages of
maps, postcards and old photos of the nostalgic
days of travel. Behind the signs of the food
establishments, the possible sihouette that a
traveller would see at nightfall.*

HAGGAR CLOTHING Co.

FRCH Design Worldwide

▲ Comfort. In the foreground, the central seating area. In the background, stools where customers can rest while paying for their purchases.

▶ The use of what seem to be unfinished items, fragments and objects out of context. Some of the furniture modules seen in this area have wooden doors at their ends. The image seems to be that of a television studio.

Coinciding with the widening of its product range and the launching of a new sales campaign, Haggar Clothing Co. opened its first shop in the spring of 1995.

The Cincinnati office of the FRCH group again uses its strategic combination of marketing and design to form an image that identifies a company with its customers.

There is no mystique about Haggar. With a lack of regard to the world of fashion, it endeavours to reflect a new approach to its clothes and its campaign.

The premises were carefully designed thinking of its clientele, the profile of which is made up of men between the ages of 25 and 49 years old who are not interested in fashion, but would like casual well-made clothes at a good price. Haggar is the latest for men who hate to go shopping or, perhaps, for the women who buy their clothes for them.

The basic space of the project could be defined as the interior of a long warehouse with a rectangular floorspace and high roof. On its walls layouts of wood and steel form shelves and hangers. On the floor, modules of low-level furniture are arranged and from the roof, lamps, posters and even dividing screens hang.

At one of the ends of the premises a storeroom is located. At the other the entrance façade is divided into two parts. One part is glazed with the doors in the middle, while the other part holds the sign with the name of the company.

The decor of the interior is based on visual elements that seem to have come from the cellar of one of its customers; bowling balls, metal drums, car number plates, old suitcases, and other household objects are laid out on the furniture and walls as if they were works of art.

The hanging lamps could also have come from someone's garage. Suspended in darkness, they define an intermediate level of lighting that makes the roof, which is already dark, with its bare structure almost invisible from floor level.

◀ *View of the entrance façade. The entrance seems to lead through to a shop where a bell rings on entering and where they stock everything.*

▶ *Detail of the furniture. They are practical, plain modules of unvarnished wood with metal corner brackets, bolts and small wheels. A veritable masterpiece in DIY.*

▼ *The atmosphere is that of a dark warehouse with hanging garage lights and advertising posters. Shelves have been built and low-level furniture fitted.*

100% cotton, wrinkle-free.
For those who like to iron we apologize.

HAGGAR
Stuff
you can wear.

Haggar Boyswear.
All kinds of
neat stuff.

HAGGAR
Stuff
you can wear.

The interior maintains the unified line of the basic space and gathers under the same surroundings casual wear, dress wear, and the ubiquitous presence of jeans. The atmosphere is quiet and relaxed.

The shop, like the clothes, also aims at being comfortable. In the centre, a seating area opens out; two armchairs, a table and a sofa on a carpet in two colours. Customers can relax in this area while they watch videoclips mixed in with Haggar advertisements. The frame of the two blue armchairs is seen, the glass table top rests on a garden hose, and the sofa is formed by the back seat of a car together with part of its chassis. The layout is located beneath an area of false ceiling with its own lighting.

Concepts with a great attractive force are brought together in this subspace; the unfinished, fragmented pieces, and objects which acquire a new use through being away

▲ *Two of the posters that make up the decor of the interior. A line of photographs and original slogans; "100% crease-resistant cotton. We apologise to those who like to iron"*

▶ *The hanging screens from the roof and the change in flooring, of natural wood and stone tiles, helps to mark out different areas.*

from their usual environment. Concepts, materialized in furniture or design, with which the consumer will identify.

The posters in the interior support the message of the campaign with the same light-hearted tone. They are part of a graphics package designed by the Cincinnati group.

It is sometimes difficult to tell the difference between what is design and what is marketing in the projects carried out by FRCH. The

▲ Old, worn-out, day-to-day items, which have been taken from their natural setting and displayed, acquire a special meaning with which the customer identifies.

▶ Elevation and transversal section. The size and positioning of posters and signs was considered very carefully. The design process blends in with the marketing campaign.

company itself uses the expression fusion to define the focus of its work. Decisions which are taken during the design process are, at the same time, a result of the campaign.

The whole shop is the result of a range of common ideas. The roof of the interior space, for example, could be the back of the armchairs. The items used in the decor are also along the same lines; the furniture can make use of the same car parts as the decor as if it were a room. ■

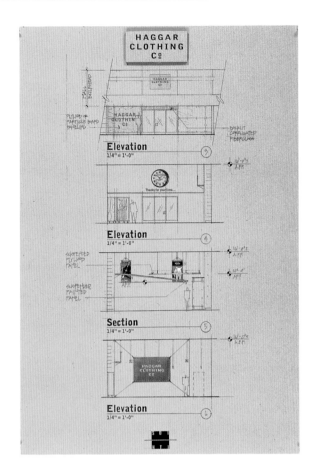

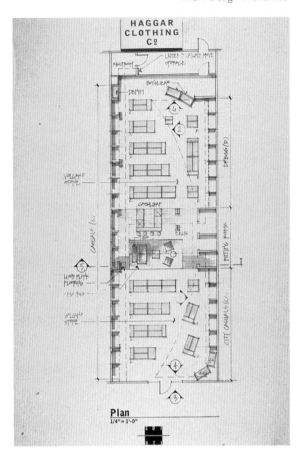

▲ *General floor plan of the project. The layout of the furniture organises movement within the shop and marks out special areas.*

▼ *Elevation of the longitudinal interiors. Between the floor and the ceiling, the lamps, screens and posters define a virtual intermediate plane.*

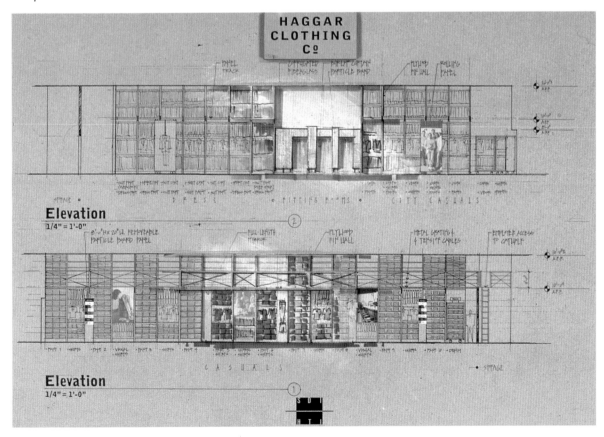

DR. BAELTZ

Shigeru Uchida

▲ View of the smaller shop, where the general lighting combines with that from the showcases to form an abstract composition in the wall.

► The abstract composition formed by the openings of different sizes in the wall behind the customer attention counter uses the containers of the Dr Baeltz brand as decorative elements.

The two cosmetic shops designed by Shigeru Uchida for Dr Baeltz represent a different approach in the design of shop premises with spaces of reduced dimensions. The different component parts of the shops have been reduced to a minimum in a process of analysis which results in an integration of a unitary design, where aesthetics blend with function.

Shigeru Uchida (Yokohama, Japan, 1943) graduated at the Kuwazawa Design School in Tokyo in 1966. In 1970, he founded the Uchida Design Studio and in 1981 he set up the present Studio 80, together with Toru Nishioka. Since the beginning of his career he has stood out in the design of furniture and various objects, as well as his work in interior design, such as the series of boutiques for Issey Miyake (1976-82), the bar Le Club (Tokyo, 1983), the hotel Il Palazzo (Fukuoka, 1991), jointly with Aldo Rossi, or the restaurant La Ranarita (Tokyo, 1991). Winner of various international prizes in design, some of

▲ View of the larger shop from outside. The counter is the only item which stands out within the general beige tones. In the background, the partition which separates the facial treatment area.

▶ Detail of the longitudinal display case in the larger shop. The case is built into a panel with a wavy wood finish, in which the plain bottles and jars of the brand stand out.

his creations form part of the permanent collections of important musems.

The philosophy behind the brand of Dr Baeltz cosmetics is based on the natural properties of their products. This factor means a different approach is required to shops of similar characteristics, where product choice depends on subjective decisions on the part of the client due to conditioning factors such as image or fashion. In Dr Baeltz shops, a beauty consultant attends the client personally and advises him or her on which type of cosmetic is appropriate in each case. This basic approach means that the two shops that we are concerned with are more spaces which relate the product to the client than display spaces. Importance does not lie with showing off the colours and textures of the product, but with enhancing its virtues by means of personal attention to the user.

Both shop premises are of reduced dimensions (29.8m and 38m) and have a

Facing the counter of the larger shop, a rectangular layout built into the wall creates a composition of shelves with their own lighting which sets off their content.

rectangular floorspace. The entrance forms part of a continuous glass façade which leads out to the shopping centre, where each of the shops is located. This gives a complete view of the interior space. The floorspace is divided into three sections; the shop, the customer attention counter and the facial treatment area at the back of the shop. The counter, located along the length of the shop and complemented by steel structure armchairs upholstered in blue, is the only item which invades the space of the premises. The products are displayed along the walls of the shop. The facial treatment area is separated from the rest of the shop by means of a partition which does not reach the ceiling, thus allowing physical and visual continuity of the space.

All of the branded products are contained in plain bottles or jars which are laid out either in display cases or shelves built into the longer walls. The display cases thus blend in with the vertical fittings. In the larger shop, a continuous narrow display case behind the counter faces a rectangular layout of shelves which takes up all of the wall. In the second shop, a random distribution of shelves of different sizes and shapes creates an abstract composition in the larger wall.

The layout of the fittings within the walls is reinforced with their own lighting which shows off the displayed products in combinations of different sizes of containers. It is thus a set-up in which display cases and products combine to produce an overall aesthetic effect.

The use of beige as the predominant colour follows a desire to enlarge the reduced space of the shops; the painted finish of the walls and ceiling, the polished marble flooring, the wavy wood finish on the panel which holds the display case in the larger shop and the glossy resin finish of the counter combine a series of tones which are brought out by a lighting system consisting of lights fitted into the false ceiling complemented by the indirect light from the display cases. ■

▼ *The longitudinal display case
built into the wall acts as a background
for the customer attention counter. It is
made up of two parts of a different
height and is situated lengthwise
in the shop.*

JOSEP FONT

Josep Font

▲ *The transparent opening of the façade means that the shop appears as a display case for the street. At night, lighting behind the shop window increases its appeal.*

► *From the entrance almost everything is seen. The walls have been painted white, the wooden flooring goes to the arch in the middle, covered with small stones. In the background, a staircase to the upper floor. (A1)*

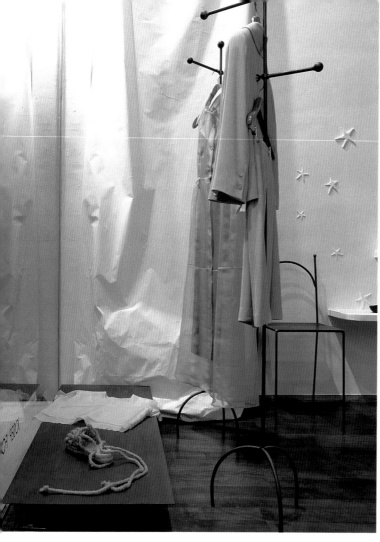

After finishing his studies of design in Barcelona, Josep Font started his professional career with Luz Diaz. The different prizes that their collections have been awarded during the second half of the eighties means the first recognition of work that has been exhibited in cities of the importance of Paris and Milan in the world of fashion.

In September, 1991 their first shop was opened at 106 Paseo de Gracia in Barcelona. A year later, their firm also set up another shop in the city of Bilbao. Both designers took on the job of decorating to the last detail their shops themselves in an attempt to follow the same lines as those of their creations in clothes.

Is it a case of the fashion designer as a decorator, interior designer, architect or even artist?

▲ The white sheet provides an effect of soft cloth shadows and crumpled paper. It forms part of the shop window and of the wall, together with the designs on the iron plate and the wrought iron stands.

▶ Subtlety in the interior. The walls offer painted white stars and shelves, the table and chair, lines, and the star and moon are in black wrought iron. (A2)

Without going into the possible connections between different artistic activities, this project is the result of how two people, used to imagining clothes now imagine spaces, two people who are used to dressing people, now dress the space for their activities and make use of materials and procedures which are different to those which are commonplace.

▼ *The staircase takes the wooden parquet upstairs. It is supported in the corner by a white column. (A3)*

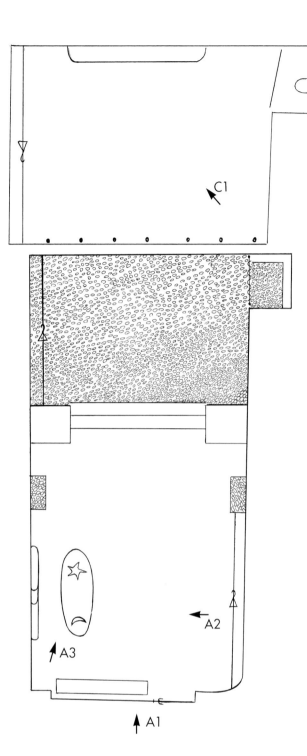

A designer's first shop means direct contact with the street. No fear was shown at this challenge and the space for displaying and showing the models designed by Josep Font and Luz Diaz opens onto the wide pavements of Paseo de Gracia. Due to the small dimensions of the premises, the shop was conceived as a display case for the street.

The opening in the facade remains empty. Only four panes of glass, one of which is the door, are seen. The largest is found to the left and corresponds to what would be a smaller shop window. The entrance door with steel hinges and supports and a double handle is located to the right and separated from the frame. The transparency is pleasing.

From the entrance almost everything is visible. The walls have been painted white. The parquet goes from the longitudinal ancient wooden beams to an arch, located midway in the shop, covered with small stones.

A white sheet hangs from the left corner of the opening. A thin iron plate seems to float at the foot of it, on which a design or accessory is displayed. Behind the iron plate, two stands of finely wrought iron hold the wooden hangers which show off two of the models. The white sheet in the corner could be a metamorphosis from the solid, flat white of the wall to a softer white of shadows and crumpled paper in an attempt to get closer to the models of the shop window. Next to the door, at the same height of the iron plate,

▲ *Approximate floorplans of the lower and upper levels. The fitting rooms of the lower level and the washroom of the higher level are included in the rectangular perimeter which forms the floorspace.*

▶ *Upper level; wooden beams, brick domes, the arch covered with stones, iron needles and parquet.*

almost hidden, in black on glass, is the logo
and name of Josep Font. Since 1995, he has
worked alone.

Immediately to the right of the entrance,
the first line of models on wooden hangers is
seen. The hangers are on a horizontal wrought
iron bar located between the entrance and
the arch.

From the arch the wooden flooring
continues along the stairs which lead upstairs,
while two steps lead down to the lower back

▲ *Detail of the spherical finish of the
handrail of the staircase and the
continuity between the steps and the
wooden flooring. In the background, a
mobile element within the space;
the partition. (C1)*

143

▲ *Partial view of Paseo de Gracia through the arch and between the needles of the handrail. The upper level appears to be the top shelf of a display case.*

▶ *Detail of a bannister without a handrail formed by bent needles with a spherical head.*

▲ *Detail of the partition of the*
upper level.

part of the shop. Both the handrail of the stairs and of the upper floor are defined by means of lines, loose lines which end in spherical heads, one is a simple handrail, the other a set of wavy vertical lines or, perhaps, bent pins stuck into the parquet.

To the left, between the shop window and the arch, the table-counter and a chair are located next to the wall. On the wall, white stars in relief are seen as well as three staggered shelves. The glass table top rests on

a star and a moon, both of wrought iron, with three legs which fix it to the floor. All of the elements of the interior either seem to be part of the wall or a set of wrought iron lines in space. The simplicity is pleasing.

On the left-hand wall on both floors are more supports for hangers. At the back of the shop the relief of the wall predominates.

The flooring of the upper level is also wood. The beams in the ceiling as well, only that they are transverse in this case. Between the beams, bricks form ceramic domes. On the parquet, a patterned white screen stands out.

The flooring of the lower level is different. According to the designers, the rough river stones try to give the effect that one is in the court of a country house. The walls are sunk back to form two shelves on which stand two items which add a personal touch; a plantpot with a flower and the carving of a Saint.

The floorspace of the premises is almost rectangular and completely free of obstructions on both of its levels except for the back right-hand corner, where there is a small square space which is the fitting room on the lower level and a small washroom upstairs.

An arch in the corner separates the fitting room from the "court". Lighting, the shelf with the plantpot, the two chairs resting against the wall, a flower traced in black lines on the floor and the lights sunk into the ceiling give this part of the shop a special atmosphere which could be confused with outdoors. The harmony is pleasing.

The aim was to offer the general public a minimalist design both in terms of space and clothes, a subtle, elegant, luminous atmosphere with a simplicity of lines and a balance between the different materials. It has been accomplished.

The basic raw material used was the white of the walls and light. Wrought iron is used and displayed as if it were a needle and thread. The concept of the space as a display case for the street is pleasing. ▪

> View of the arch in the corner of the fitting room entrance. The lighting of its interior and that of the shelf where the plantpot is located create a special atmosphere of lights and shadows on the white walls. (B1)

◄ Corner of the "court" consisting of a floor made up of river stones. Again, wrought iron lines form the stand, the chair and the flower.

◄ The relief of the walls, showing the shape of a star or two sunken shelves. One, in shadow, holds a Saint, while the other, illuminated, a flower.

▼ Detail of the fitting room with the curtain in the entrance, within its white interior a seat and cushion.

OCKY'S

Torsten Neeland

▲ *Both the furniture as well as the materials or the lighting of the denim-wear shop Ocky's in Hamburg try to give the premises an austere, simple image but, at the same time concise and powerful.*

► *View of the shelves in the form of cubic boxes located opposite the entrance. Both the space between the floor and the first box as well as the spaces beween each one means a change in the logic of the gravity that gives a greater force to these elements. (A1)*

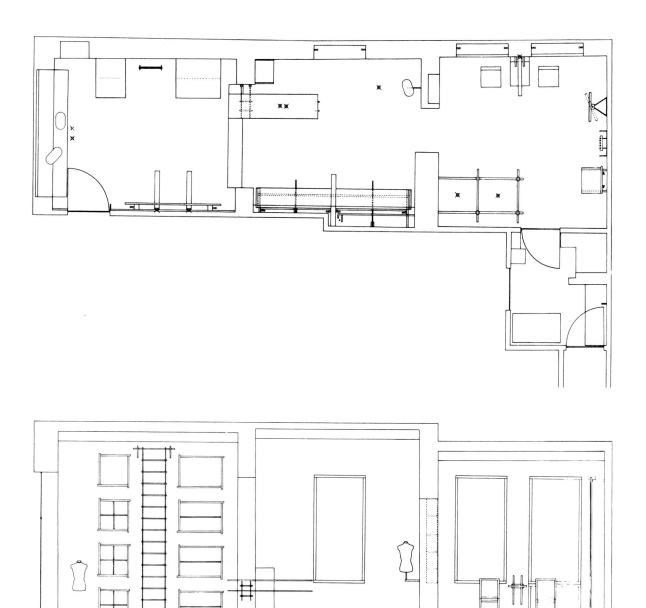

▲ General floor plan of the premises and longitudinal section. As can be seen, due to the reduced width of the rooms, the height of the ceilings gives a special character to the premises.

▲ Detail of the shop window. The main opening to the street has been glazed with the logo of the shop in the centre. The entrance is located in the adjacent side door.

Ocky's is a chain of denim-wear shops that is well established in Germany. The premises designed by the young designer Torsten Neeland is situated in Harburg, an area of Hamburg, the important port in the north of Germany. The premises is located on the ground floor of a building constructed in 1905. It is a small shop, approximately 45m², that was previously a baker's. The state of conservation was not particularly good which meant that the premises needed complete reforms before a clothes chop could be set up there.

The space is of a rectangular character, the façade is narrow and the shop opens out towards the interior in a series of three chambers, separated by supporting walls. Each one of these subspaces has a narrow area which reduces their possibilities of being used as display and storage areas. However, the ceilings are relatively high, up to 4.30 m, as

151

well as the doors, which are 3m high. The first two rooms are used for display and storage, while the last one is used for the fitting rooms. Neeland has fitted very few elements in each one of them, a counter, a mannequin, a mirror, a hanger...

In spite of the reduced size of the space, Torsten Neeland has managed to reduce the claustrophobic feeling so typical of small, colourful premises. Instead of trying to make use of the space to the maximum by squeezing objects in, the German designer has managed to make each element an isolated entity, by giving it an individual identity, a specific role within the whole and the surrounding space.

The way Torsten Neeland conceives space approaches the work of minimalist sculptors. Some of the elements that are found in the Hamburg establishment of Ocky's, such as the cubic ash shelves which hang from the wall of the first room, recall the work of the North-American artist, Donald Judd. Neeland explores the possibilities of simple geometries. Any superfluous element is removed from the space and objects acquire an unknown relevance, an open force that seems to arise from its simplicity. The furniture, designed by Torsten Neeland is both forceful and austere,

◀ *General view of the establishment from the counter. Although the premises is made up of the same space, it is divided into different ambits with distinct functions; the storage and display area, the sales area and the fitting rooms. (B1)*

▶ *The materials and colours used for the finishes are of a great simplicity.*

◄ Detail of the counter area. A galvanized steel fixed in the wall supports two thick glass plates that project out. A polished glass plate fitted into the wall with fluorescent tubes in the interior provides illumination.

► The wooden boxes that are used as shelves are hung in a series of identical units, of which the highest is at an angle to the others. These elements somehow recall some of the minimalist compositions of Donald Judd. (A2)

► Detail of a bar with hangers located opposite the counter. The singular design of the hangers has been done by Torsten Neeland, as well as the rest of the furniture. In this case, the bending of a galvanised steel has provided a hanger.

◄ Detail of a shelf in the fitting room area. Although the furniture is designed with extraordinarily simple forms, the thickness of the components is considerable such that the objects have both a solid and robust presence.

► Detail of the element that supports the two glass plates that make up the counter.

▶ The galvanized steel objects introduce industrial aesthetics within the shop, a look of heavy machinery, that takes its reference from the landscape of the port in the city of Hamburg where the establishment is located.

▼ A chair is the only mobile element in all of the shop except for the clothes. To a certain extent, not only the walls, the partitions, the floor and the doors but also all of the wooden, steel and glass objects shape the architecture.

of pure forms, perfect cubes from which perfect spaces are removed, constructed with unworked materials, of a considerable thickness, and simple joints. However, there are small alterations, slight shifts of planes with respect to others that introduce impure subtleties in the absolute form, giving both mystery and secrecy to pieces that were previously recognisable.

On the other hand, each element forms part of a global conception of the space. The cubic shelves are repeated, thus establishing a network in which slight, almost imperceptible variations are seen. This dialogue between the different elements taughtens the space, giving it an extra force.

The individual objects, such as the counter, the mirror or each one of the hangers have been especially designed for this establishment. They are unique pieces. As Neeland points out; "precisely by unique elements and love for detail, an intensity is created which adds to the concept of form a more individual character and a great persuading force."

Many people may consider the rigour of Torten Neeland's work disproportionate, his care for detail excessive, the conceptual considerations undertaken by the young German designer unnecessary, taking into account that we are talking about a commercial establishment and not an artistic environment, that so much care taken in the choice of the elements is for a place that is destined to the

sale of jeans and that the clients are probably
more concerned about price than the
character of the space. It is a fallacy based on
ease and laziness and, in the end, a trap.
There is nothing more necessary for a shop
than to possess its own identity which makes
it both recognisable and memorable.
Establishments which are imprecise are
condemned to oblivion. ▩

▲ *Overhead view of the fitting
rooms. The curtains of the rooms are seen
in the mirror. (C1)*

► **MICHAEL GABELLINI**

- Studies at The Rhode Island School of Design, 1980, and at the Architectural Association in London.
- 6 years at the arctitectural studio, Kohn Petersen Fox Associates.
- In 1987 Gabellini Associates is founded, together with Jake Smith, devoted to the design of boutiques, detached houses, temporary exhibitions and furniture.

► **EDUARD SAMSÓ**

- Barcelona, 1956.
- Architect, industrial and interior designer. Studies between 1973 and 1980 (Esc. de Arquitectura del Vallès).
- FAD prize (Fomento de las Artes Decorativas) for the best interior in 1985 and 1986. The FAD prize for interior design in 1987 and the EDIM prize in 1988 for the best interior of the Community of Madrid.
- Public recognition (radio, television, books and specialized international reviews).

► **THOMPSON, VENTULETT, SATINBACK & ASSOCIATES.**

- Studio founded in Atlanta (Georgia), 1969.
- Architects and interior designers.
- Main projects; Long Beach Convention Center, the Omni Arena and Georgia Dome stdiums, the Georgia World Congress Center and the buildings of the Concourse Complex.

► **STUDIO GRANDA**

- Reykjavik (Iceland), 1987.
- Founded by Steve Christer and Margret Harðardóttir.
- Studies at the Universities of Newcastle and Edinburgh. they have received numerous prizes and awards, especially the nomination for the prestigious "Mies van der Rohe" prize for European architecture.

► **RON ARAD**

- Tel Aviv (Israel), 1951.
- Established in London since 1973, studies at the Architectural Association School of Architecture until 1979.
- In 1981, together with Dennis Groves and Caroline Thorman, he set up his place of work, exhibition and sale of furniture, One Off.
- Architect, manufacturer of furniture, Horns Collection (1986), interior architect, "Bazaar", for Gaultier, designer, Volumes Collection (1988) form part of his singular work.

► **FRCH DESIGN WORLDWIDE**

- New York, 1968.
- Offices in Cincinnati, New York and Singapore.
- They have received more than 150 awards and the recognition of prestigious institutions.
- Multidisciplinary activity. Main areas of work; architecture, construction, interior design, lighting, graphic communication, project management.